Praise for *The Financial Business Development*

'Ian Cooper points out the blindingly obvious to managers who seem to run their businesses with their eyes shut and ears covered. His book is packed with jaw-dropping anecdotes of opportunities lost and custom going begging because suppliers of goods and services have forgotten who their customers are and what they actually want. Ian does not preach or hector but his insights into how business is getting it wrong act as a powerful catalyst to help businesses of all sizes improve and develop in a tough climate. His message is delivered with his usual gentle humour that occasionally spills over into downright exasperation.'

Len Tingle, BBC Political Editor – Yorkshire, veteran
BBC broadcaster and writer on business issues

'This simple no-nonsense approach to business development provides a recipe for success for any business, regardless of size.'

Wendy Atkin-Smith, Managing Director,
Viking River Cruises UK Limited

'Considered, down to earth and straight to the point. This guide is a true testament to Ian Cooper's knowledgeable and no-nonsense approach.'

Brett Dennis – Marketing strategist for Every1

'This is a game changer for any business wishing to grow and develop. Ian Cooper has a phenomenal understanding of the importance of delivering world class service to your clients and customers. I will encourage all members of the 360 legal group to purchase and treat this as their mantra!'

Viv Williams, CEO, 360 Legal Group

'*The Financial Times Guide to Business Development* is thoroughly readable and no-nonsense, with immediately usable advice on every page. It is classic Ian Cooper ... clear, concise and common sense.'

Chris Spencer, General Counsel, EMIS Group plc

'It is worth getting this book for the 21 common sense business development truths alone. Painfully brutal in places, these truths should serve as a much needed wake up call, and I have never met a business that wouldn't benefit from applying them honestly to their situation. Ian Cooper has done UK Ltd a great service by spelling them out with such clarity, simplicity and power.'

Steve Pipe FCA, author of The UK's best accountancy
practices *and* Stress proof your business and your life
and former UK Entrepreneur of the Year

'I thought I knew business development inside out. Then I read this witty, informative and practical book, and realised how much I didn't know. If you have a business that needs a boost, then it shows how anyone can become a ninja at business development.'

Heather Townsend, author of **The Financial Times Guide to Business Networking**

'This book serves as a salient reminder that your business is failing if it doesn't treat the customer as king in all it does. Packed with amusing anecdotes and practical tips, everyone in business would benefit from the lessons it provides. I challenge anyone to read this book and not find at least one area they can improve.'

Craig Holt, Chief Executive, QualitySolicitors

'We have used Ian Cooper's considerable skills on many occasions and he has shown us how to increase our conversion rate of enquiries to business from 30% to 75%. His new book, *The Financial Times Guide to Business Development* is almost a pocket book guide to his training, providing a real focus on how to get results. It not only explains what to do, but why, in an entertaining, pragmatic and anecdotal style.'

Martyn Morgan, Managing Partner, QualitySolicitors Talbots

The Financial Times Guide to Business Development

PEARSON

At Pearson, we believe in learning – all kinds of learning for all kinds of people. Whether it's at home, in the classroom or in the workplace, learning is the key to improving our life chances.

That's why we're working with leading authors to bring you the latest thinking and the best practices, so you can get better at the things that are important to you. You can learn on the page or on the move, and with content that's always crafted to help you understand quickly and apply what you've learned.

If you want to upgrade your personal skills or accelerate your career, become a more effective leader or more powerful communicator, discover new opportunities or simply find more inspiration, we can help you make progress in your work and life.

Pearson is the world's leading learning company. Our portfolio includes the Financial Times, Penguin, Dorling Kindersley, and our educational business, Pearson International.

Every day our work helps learning flourish, and wherever learning flourishes, so do people.

To learn more please visit us at: **www.pearson.com/uk**

The Financial Times Guide to Business Development

How to win profitable customers and clients

Ian Cooper

Harlow, England • London • New York • Boston • San Francisco • Toronto • Sydney • Auckland • Singapore • Hong Kong
Tokyo • Seoul • Taipei • New Delhi • Cape Town • São Paulo • Mexico City • Madrid • Amsterdam • Munich • Paris • Milan

Pearson Education Limited

Edinburgh Gate
Harlow CM20 2JE
Tel: +44 (0)1279 623623
Fax: +44 (0)1279 431059
Website: www.pearson.com/uk

First published in Great Britain in 2012

© Ian Cooper 2012

The right of Ian Cooper to be identified as author of this work has been asserted by him in
accordance with the Copyright, Designs and Patents Act 1988.

Pearson Education is not responsible for the content of third-party internet sites.

ISBN: 978-0-273-75953-9

British Library Cataloguing-in-Publication Data
A catalogue record for this book is available from the British Library

Library of Congress Cataloging-in-Publication Data
Cooper, Ian.
   The Financial times guide to business development : how to win profitable
customers and clients / Ian Cooper.
      p. cm.
   Includes index.
   ISBN 978-0-273-75953-9 (limp)
   1.   Business planning.   I. Title.
   HD30.28.C6632 2012
   658.4'01--dc23
                                    2012008814

All rights reserved. No part of this publication may be reproduced, stored in a retrieval system,
or transmitted in any form or by any means, electronic, mechanical, photocopying, recording
or otherwise, without either the prior written permission of the publisher or a licence
permitting restricted copying in the United Kingdom issued by the Copyright Licensing
Agency Ltd, Saffron House, 6–10 Kirby Street, London EC1N 8TS. This book may not be lent,
resold, hired out or otherwise disposed of by way of trade in any form of binding or cover
other than that in which it is published, without the prior consent of the Publishers.

All trademarks used herein are the property of their respective owners. The use of any
trademark in this text does not vest in the author or publisher any trademark ownership
rights in such trademarks, nor does the use of such trademarks imply any affiliation with or
endorsement of this book by such owners.

The Financial Times. With a worldwide network of highly respected journalists, *The
Financial Times* provides global business news, insightful opinion and expert analysis
of business, finance and politics. With over 500 journalists reporting from 50 countries
worldwide, our in-depth coverage of international news is objectively reported and
analysed from an independent, global perspective. To find out more, visit
www.ft.com/pearsonoffer.

10 9 8 7 6 5 4 3 2
16 15 14 13 12

Typeset in 9/13pt ITC Stone Serif Std by 3
Printed and bound by Ashford Colour Press, Gosport

To my kids ... Samantha, Howard, David and the next generation ... they make all the business development efforts worthwhile!

Contents

Acknowledgements

I would like to express my sincere gratitude to the many people who have played a part in influencing and shaping this project.

To Liz Gooster who first approached me about writing this book; Elie Williams from Pearson for all her skilful input and clarity of understanding; and Heather Townsend, author of *The Financial Times Guide to Business Networking*, for her patient advice on social media topics ... my grateful and sincere thanks. Additional thanks for their skill, patience and input to Helen Savill, Linda Dhondy, Viv Church, Lucy Carter, Anna Jackson and Isobel McLean who make up the Pearson team.

I would also like to say a big thank you to Wendy Atkin-Smith from Viking River Cruises, Gary Book from the Leeds Building Society, Jonathan Straight of Straight plc, Craig Holt from QualitySolicitors, Mario Fijalkowski of Coronos Playa Hotel, Lanzarote, Michael McInerney of the Merton Hotel, Jersey and Sara Kahn of Sharkey's Cuts for Kids, all of whom were generous with their time, comments and strategies. My thanks too to John Goodman of US-based TARP Worldwide for permission to use some of its research information.

On a much more personal level, yet again I want to publicly say a huge thank you to my wife Helene, for all her endless encouragement, love, patience and practical support during my time working on this project.

An opening bit of food for thought!

Knowing something, isn't the same as deciding to do something!

Deciding to do something, isn't the same as actually doing it!

Doing it, isn't the same as doing it well!

Ian Cooper

Introduction

In September 2010 I got an e-mail from my publishers, which read, 'Ian, I wonder if you might be interested in writing *The Financial Times Guide to Business Development*? If so let's have a chat.' Despite being a little flattered by the idea, believe it or not the rational part of my brain screamed out, 'No ... not again.' I'd written several books before, done the early morning writing shifts and promised my wife, myself, my computer-typing finger and my bad back that I had quit. As you can see, however, the temptation was too great!

I started to ask myself why I should write such a book. What could I contribute that was really different? What do business readers really want? After spending several weeks thinking about these questions and asking many business people about their likes and dislikes in existing business development information, I eventually took up the offer of a 'chat' and explained my concept. If I were to go ahead, I said, I would produce a business development success book with a difference. I wanted to write one that would:

- be engaging, down to earth and entertaining to read and full of simple, commonsense pragmatism, rather than just academic business theory;

- inspire aspirational readers from businesses of all sizes and sectors to be 'more profitable' rather than just 'better educated and smarter';

- provide some real step-by-step priorities, tools and usable techniques;

- have a realistic regard for business development spending power, as many readers from small businesses simply want to know how to make a little budget go a long way;

- be provocative, honest and challenging where needed;

- highlight real examples of outstanding business development practice in action and also flag up examples of plain commercial silliness to avoid;

- be well structured so that it could either be read in individual sections or viewed as a whole;

- motivate, inspire and act as a catalyst for really effective action;

- 'join the dots' between other specialist books. (My research showed that most business development books focus on specific topics. I wanted to create one that would be comprehensive and pull all the major issues together into one publication.)

Luckily, the publishers were happy to go along with my vision and so my early morning writing shifts began again ... as did my aching back!

Jump forward to the present and you now have the opportunity to read *The Financial Times Guide to Business Development: How to win profitable customers and clients*, the most comprehensive collection of commonsense business development techniques ever, all brought together into one book.

Regardless of your business sector or size, whether you are a budding entrepreneur, existing business owner, manager or director, or an individual providing a service of some sort, this is 'the' definitive business development 'how to' book. It's aimed at busy, ambitious business people who make decisions, have to live with the consequences of their results and are hungry for more revenue, profits and business success.

I am 100 per cent confident that you will find this book engaging, provocative and informative, and that if you follow the steps you will automatically experience massive improvements in your business development results.

Read, understand, smile and take effective action!

1

The 21 commonsense business development truths

As readers of this book you will be preoccupied with questions such as these:

- How do we win more customers or clients?
- How do we generate more profit with a small or limited budget?
- How can we develop our business without having to win any new customers or clients?
- Why is it that our competitors seem to be doing better than us?
- What do we have to do to be more successful?

Let me be very clear about this from the outset. This book is not just about winning brand new customers. In my business development world, it is also very much about getting existing customers and clients to do more business with you and maximising the commercial leads and business opportunities that you already have. With this in mind many sections of the book are devoted to these issues.

By the time you have read and digested more than 650 tips, techniques, key questions and supportive tools in this book, you will have the answers to all the questions above and know what to do to get bigger and better results. However, before you start there is one other fundamental thing you must understand about this subject and my approach to it.

Business development is about much more than just marketing, sales, pitching, online wizardry, mailings, advertising, branding, social media strategies, glossy brochures, discount deals, promotional gimmicks or special events. Every single thing a business does has a potential impact on business development. You are doing it all the time. You shouldn't be thinking 'Today I'll do some business development, but tomorrow I'll focus on some other aspect of the business.' It is all part of the same process with the shared objective of moving your business forward towards its targeted commercial objectives.

Whatever your size or sector, if you have HR people, an operations department, a helpline support unit, a training team, members of staff who help out part time answering your phone, customer services and complaints folk, retail assistants or other support staff ... they are all in reality part of your business development team. Yes, their job description might say something else, but they all represent you and your business in some way. If you want to develop your business, win more profitable customers and clients and keep them coming back for more, then you must understand the importance of this integration. You must also make absolutely sure that everyone in your organisation knows it too and realises the very real contribution that they make to your overall success.

All your staff need to appreciate with total clarity that it is your customers and clients – actually *their* customers and clients – who ultimately pay their wages, and not you.

This is just one of many simple business development essentials that can sometimes be overlooked by the smartest and most creative business development people working in the fast-paced cut and thrust of daily business life.

With this concept in mind, before we look at a whole range of practical business development and business winning activities, which will answer all the questions above and give you the results you are looking for, I want to address what I call the *21 commonsense business development truths*. These are the basics you must have in place.

It's as simple as this: the more of these 'truths' you are getting right, the more successful you will be and, conversely, the more of these you are falling down on, the more business you will fail to win. After these basic truths, almost everything else is mere detail. They are the ingredients of your business development success recipe.

I make no apologies for how obvious, simple and even clichéd some of these truths are. After 31 years of working with over 800 businesses, I can tell you, it isn't only what you know on an intellectual level that counts, it's also about whether your business is actually doing the things that you know it should be, on the 'front line'. As I go through these commonsense 'truths' in an observational and anecdotal way, and as you smile and empathise with many of the situations and scenarios, I urge you to keep an open and honest mind and seriously consider these questions:

- ▓ Could that be us?
- ▓ Are we actually doing what we know?
- ▓ How can we tell if we have a problem in these areas?
- ▓ What can we do to put things right?
- ▓ How much are we losing each year that we could win?

So, let's get going with the 21 truths.

1. Focus on converting leads, not just on generating them

Partners in a law firm attending a seminar of mine told me that for just one of their services they had attracted 586 telephone enquiries from potential clients in the previous year through their costly business development activities. However, they explained, they turned only 13 per cent into business and they were losing money. What did they do about this? They asked me to help them with their business development … to generate more enquiries!

Instead I encouraged them to re-define their priorities and to look at how their enquiries were dealt with. Here is what I found: the enquiries were dealt with badly, by bored untrained staff, who treated potential clients as though they were a nuisance. The callers, who were often emotionally distressed, were processed through a largely irrelevant legal administrative questionnaire that neither caller nor call handler fully understood.

There was no real conversation, no rapport built up or interest shown in the caller's situation. No helpful information was offered, little follow-up was done and not one of the call handlers thought to ask if the potential client wanted to go ahead. The only surprising thing is that they got as much as a 13 per cent conversion rate. I guess some callers were just plain desperate.

I was able to help the partners in the firm recognise that the real problem was not their lack of leads but the total absence of attention and focus on the efficient and effective handling of enquiries. I showed them a new and proper structure for this, changed the methods of call handling and gave the relevant personnel some guidance and training.

Six months later, with no money spent at all on external business development or marketing activities, this legal practice was converting 82 per cent of exactly the same type of enquiries into profitable business. In financial terms this was worth an extra £404,340 per year.

How much are you losing each year by overlooking this commonsense truth?

I will be looking in much more detail at this issue later in the book and providing special techniques and guidance which have the potential to give you some equally massive improvements (see Chapter 5).

2. Exceed customer or client expectations

Let me ask you a really simple question. Can you instantly name three occasions in your life when an organisation you've done business with has massively exceeded your expectations? I don't just mean delivered on its promises and done a good job, but consciously given you a positive and excited feeling that it has gone way past what you expected.

Have you immediately got three names in your head? Actually have you got one?

Despite the clichéd mantra of many corporate leaders and executives, that 'we strive to exceed customer expectations', when I have asked people this question, very few have quickly been able to come up with three really great examples.

To be blunt, it is a business development truth that exceeding customer or client expectations is not as common as it should be, regardless of the fact that it really is the holy grail of sustained business success. If, as a business, you can consistently exceed customer/client expectations, then subject to market factors you are able to charge premium prices in your sector, get very high levels of repeat business and fantastic word-of-mouth referrals.

By the way, I can't immediately think of three answers either, but I can think of one. My wife and I recently took a holiday to China with a company called Viking River Cruises. No prizes for guessing what business they are in! Not only was the overall trip as good as we had hoped, but it totally exceeded our wildest expectations in every possible respect and was an absolute 'masterclass' in customer service. This was not just my opinion, I spoke to a very large number of other passengers who felt exactly the same.

Now before I get too carried away sharing my personal holiday experiences, my interest as a business writer is in how Viking River Cruises manages to achieve what so few businesses are able to do. What is the strategic thinking and activity that makes these high business aspirations a reality? What lessons can other businesses of all types learn from Viking? With these questions in mind I spoke to the company's UK managing director Wendy Atkin-Smith.

She gave me several answers, all of which can be conceptually modelled:

- ■ 'We track feedback on everything, even the small details. For example, we spent a huge amount of time recently just reviewing and discussing the quality and appearance of our crockery and cutlery.'

- ■ 'We deliberately don't oversell in our brochures, in fact we consciously undersell. We want people to be surprised when they get even more than they had expected.'

- ■ 'We find the best people, look after them and pay them well. Excellence starts with recruitment. We identify people at the outset who are prepared to go the extra mile.'

- ■ 'We like to keep control over every aspect of what we do and we never give anything out to third parties. All elements are controlled and staffed by Viking River Cruises trained people, even if they are based locally.'

- ■ 'The overall Viking ethos is about exceeding customer expectations and in training we are massively passionate about customer service.'

There are two other factors I would like to mention that show how seriously this company takes this issue and commitment. Firstly it communicates and builds its aims into its branding. With its registered strap line, Viking River Cruises ... The World's Leading River Cruise Line ... By Far®, it immediately and very publicly establishes, both externally and internally, high standards to achieve. If you set such standards and targets in the first place, you are more likely to achieve them than by setting no standards!

I was also intrigued and impressed with the passenger feedback sheets given out at the end of the trip. Gone were the usual questions and boxes to tick, inviting holidaymakers to select excellent, good, average or poor. The whole of Viking's evaluation process was based around questions that matched its branding and ethos. Viking asks passengers to indicate whether the experience was 'far above expectations', 'above expectations', 'as expected', etc.

What can you learn from all this that you can use in your own business development? (See Chapter 6, golden rule 2 for advice on getting your service standards right.)

3. Speak to potential customers or clients ... and speak to them nicely

Picture the scene. After several years of driving the same car that was getting worn out and cranky (a bit like its owner), I decided it was time for a change. So off I went car shopping. I went to four dealerships in the space of one morning. Between them, all of these manufacturers spend millions trying to get prospective car buyers like me to think about them and then to go and look at their vehicles. Here's what happened.

Dealer 1 told me, 'We have a special promotional event on this weekend so we can't spend much time with you ... but you can have a glass of champagne.' Not a total waste of time then!

Dealers 2 and 3 ignored me totally. Although I walked around the showroom and forecourt in my most interested, potential car buying manner, getting in and out of cars and reading information and price labels, astonishingly, nobody approached me. After a full 15 minutes at each dealership none of the salespeople had spoken to me at all. This was despite the fact that in both dealerships there were at least three sales executives sitting alone at their impressive desks with a pile of business cards in front of them, no doubt doing something important.

At dealer 4's showroom I must have made customer service sales history. I got thrown out of its showroom trying to buy a car! Yes ... I was shown the 'red card'. What was my crime? Did I try to steal a car or spill my lunch over the plush leather seating? No, here is what happened and how the conversation went.

'How much is that car over there? There is no price on the windscreen.'

'Sold,' came back the reply.

'How about that one then?'

'Sold,' he replied again as he turned to walk off back to his desk.

'Perhaps you could take my contact details down, with what I am looking for, so you could get back to me when you have something that matches,' I very politely and helpfully suggested.

'I don't need you to tell me how to do my job … just get out,' he shouted aggressively, pointing to the door.

Guess what? I didn't need telling twice. I did leave, but it won't surprise you to know that when I did eventually buy a vehicle, it was not of course from him or that dealership. Nevertheless, he wins the prize for being the best salesman of my car buying morning. Unlike the other dealers, at least he made conversation with me … well, all 17 words of it. The only problem was that two of them were 'get out'!

Remember, 'people buy people' first. What are yours like at dealing with your customers and clients?

Now let me give you a positive example of how to get things right and the impact this can have on business development.

> My wife and I were considering which of many financial organisations to choose for a particular bit of business. We had dealt with many in the past with varying degrees of satisfaction. After several telephone calls, which had us selecting endless recorded options, being put on 'hold' for an unacceptable amount of time, being grilled excessively with security questions, only to be put through to people who were unhelpful and who lacked product knowledge or communications skills, we tried the Leeds Building Society. Here is what happened.

The number we dialled connected us immediately with a real person at the branch. The young woman we spoke to was helpful, clear and instantly able to answer our questions knowledgeably. As a result, we arranged to call in that morning to discuss taking things further with her and she told us what we would need to bring with us.

On arrival, though she was busy with another customer, she politely excused herself for a moment to greet us and introduced us to the branch manager who was available to help.

He was friendly, had excellent interpersonal skills, was respectful, asked the right questions, made us feel like he was interested in doing business with us, had good knowledge of his product range, was able to answer our questions without jargon and put no needless obstacles in the way. The result: we did business with the Leeds Building Society and now we tell others how excellent it is.

Though the manager's job description probably doesn't mention business development in any formal sense, everything he and his colleagues did is a great example of business development. Gary Brook, Head of Corporate Communication at the Leeds Building Society, talks about how this way of dealing with customers is 'embedded in our culture'. To ensure that the good intentions are translated into sustained standards he explained:

'The Society carries out a number of external exercises to monitor service, obtain feedback and understand customer sentiment. These include mystery shop exercises, independent customer surveys, staff opinion surveys, product surveys and a range of forums including those for branch managers on the issue of treating customers fairly.'

For more information on what you can do, see Chapter 6, golden rule 2.

4. Be open for business

The managing director of a successful business told me recently how he rang a five star hotel, part of a major chain, that considered itself to be one of the most elegant and luxurious hotels in London, to make a reservation.

He was told by a receptionist to whom he got through that: 'Reservation staff don't work on Sundays so you can't book today.' End of call!

'I booked with another hotel,' he told me.

Let's get this straight. This is a nonsense. I don't know what this organisation's promotional budget is, but it seems to me that turning away people who actively want to spend money with it, then and there, makes a mockery out of its business development efforts and spend.

The basic questions then are: how do your opening hours impact on your business? What do you do to cover lunch and breaks? What time do you close in the evening? When do your potential customers or clients want to contact you and do business? What do your competitors do? How can you adapt to the buying habits of your customers or clients?

These are serious business development issues. Don't ignore them. I am, of course, aware of and sympathetic to internal lunchtime staffing rotas, the logistical problems faced by small and growing businesses and the 'work–life' balance issue. However, it is undeniable that accessibility and availability are basic business development truths. If you are closed when your customers and clients want to buy from you, don't be surprised if you lose business to your competitors who are open for business.

5. Don't let your admin get in the way

I recently took a phone call from the conference manager of a major hotel chain … a brand name that everyone in the world would recognise. This manager wanted me to complete an administrative form relating to how I would pay for an event that I was speaking at, which my seminar business was organising and holding in his hotel. Unfortunately I was travelling and thus unable to complete the form then and there. As a result of this the manager seemed overcome with an administrative spasm. 'I need that form and we can't go ahead with the event without it,' he said. Here is the rest of the conversation in summary:

'No problem,' I said. 'To give you total peace of mind, although I can't complete the form right now, I'll pay everything upfront with my credit card, so you don't need to worry about it.'

'No, it's not about getting the money … it's about getting the form back.'

'I understand that, and as soon as I get back to the office later this evening I will complete all the paperwork and send it through to you. Actually, right now getting all the money in advance is even better for you than the paperwork.'

'The money is not important to me,' he said.

How many of your people tell customers and clients that paying 'is not important'?

The fact of the matter is that every business, regardless of its size, will have its administrative processes, procedures and systems. That is absolutely fine, indeed it makes sense to do whatever is necessary to streamline the delivery of service. However, where the processing becomes more important than the commercial objectives of the business itself, then there is a problem.

In this instance the conference manager was purely task driven about getting back his form. To him this process was more important than getting paid.

Remember, you are not in business to fulfil and justify your administrative tasks. They are merely a stepping-stone to more important goals.

6. There's no job more important than helping customers or clients part with their cash!

One of my seminar delegates, a company director, shared a recent clothes shopping experience with me. She told me how at 4.30 pm she had walked into the fitting room of a national retail chain to try on two items of clothing. A member of staff stopped her and said, 'Sorry, you can't try those on.' 'Why not?' asked my delegate. 'Because I have other jobs to attend to here in the fitting room area before we close.'

If I was being very charitable, perhaps this might be understandable and justifiable at 4.55 pm if the store closes at 5 pm. At 4.30 pm, however, with a full half hour to go there is absolutely no justification for turning a potential customer away. Apart from any lost revenue from those purchases it does nothing for customer service.

Whatever jobs the store member of staff had to perform, nothing was more important than helping or indeed allowing a potential customer to make a purchase. Never forget, it is your customers and clients who pay the wages, and not the company.

7. Don't let technology get in the way

I once found myself in a US-style restaurant diner. I had met with a client for coffee and by 11.45 am we had pretty much finished and fancied some food. We were told we couldn't order anything, because 'We enter your choice of food onto our hand held terminals ... and the computers don't let us take orders until 12 noon.' Simple: we left and bought an early lunch elsewhere.

How often have you been faced with 'the computer is down' or 'the computer says no' excuse? How does this make you feel as a potential customer or client?

While many do what we did in this example and buy elsewhere, there are still many consumers who reluctantly accept that this is okay. It is not! Nor is it acceptable from a business point of view. If you are aware of 'technology excuses' happening in your business, then do something about it, before you lose customers.

Making use of modern technology or computer systems to enhance efficiency is to be supported, but if for any reason you have a problem with your technology or you have a customer or client who wants something outside of the norm … like an early lunch … then encourage your team to be flexible and to find a way of making it happen. For example, the diner mentioned above could have made an exception and made us the food first and generated the order afterwards, once its systems were up and running. This may have been different for the staff, but it would certainly have been more profitable than saying no.

If you are an owner or a manager, empower your staff to use their initiative to stop technology being an obstacle to doing business.

8. Quality and word-of-mouth count for everything

A restaurant owner acquired new premises in a fantastic location. He spent a huge sum fitting it out with beautiful furnishings and décor and created a wonderfully comprehensive menu, which was appropriately themed and tastefully printed. Everything was polished and brand spanking new, ready for the big launch. There had been lots of promotion to get diners in during the opening few weeks and there was a real buzz of expectation locally. Everything was perfect, except for just two things … the quality of the food and the service.

Everyone who went there had a bad experience. Negative word of mouth was the norm. Stories were told of inefficient service, long waits, items on the menu not available, mistakes made over orders and finally food poisoning. As a business, the restaurant did not last long.

Despite all the preparation and cosmetic attention to the décor and premises, ultimately the poor quality of the product and service contributed to the demise of this restaurant and indeed the owner's business aspirations.

The moral of the story is simple. If you want to be successful you have to be absolutely committed to quality. It isn't enough to pay lip service to it. It has to be of paramount importance. Forget business development activities altogether if you have a lousy product or service.

One other point, don't ever assume your quality is fine because few people formally complain. Trust me, most people don't communicate their dissatisfaction to the business. They simply don't come back for more and they tell lots of other people how bad you were … and then these people tell others as well. The answer of course is to actively invite feedback. (See Chapter 6, golden rule 2.)

9. Actively strive for consistency

How often have you commented that a business you have dealt with in the past has lost its way and that its overall standards have slipped?

This is a familiar cry, particularly in the current economic climate where many businesses are cutting corners to save cash. It is a business development truth however that 'standards consistency' can be achieved with limited financial investment if the corporate mindset is correct. In most cases it is a product of internal thinking, strong leadership and personal commitment from the top. Let me give you one great example of this.

I have visited a particular hotel many times over the past 12 years ... The Merton Hotel in Jersey. It has always impressed me, not just with its high standards, but particularly for the way it has consistently maintained them over the years in the face of a very tough economy. While many businesses have fought a losing battle with this issue of consistency, the Merton has not let its standards drop. How have they done it? I asked their general manager, Michael McInerney, to share his thinking and secrets. Here is a sample of what he said:

'If you want consistency, you have to have a consistent team and to do that you have to look after your staff and make them feel valued. If you do this they will be interested in the business and look after your customers.

'One of the ways we get consistency is through the management team actively engaging with customers. Even though it takes extra time, I am a visible and accessible presence around the hotel. In general terms, management these days seem to have lost the art of looking customers in the eye. Because I am always around and interacting with people, I regularly pick up feedback about anything that might need fixing.'

Many businesses could learn a lot from this approach. What can you do to make your staff feel great about working for you and how can you engage more with your customers and clients to get closer to them? (See Chapter 6 for many examples of this.)

10. Recruitment is part of business development

A colleague and I were asked to review the way a major package holiday company employed and recruited its staff. We had the enlightening experience of sitting in on the group interview sessions as it recruited a number of reps who looked after children for their Spanish holidays.

We encountered during these sessions a very bright and personable young woman who spoke fluent Spanish, had lots of relevant experience, the necessary child care certifications and qualifications and yet she got turned down. At the same time, we witnessed other candidates, who were far less appropriate and qualified, being offered jobs. We privately asked the HR team carrying out the recruitment why such an obviously strong and perfect applicant had been rejected. Their answer was astonishing: 'We don't have any company uniform blouses that go up to a size 18. The only sizes we have are 8 to 16.'

This is an almost unbelievable example of commercial and business insanity. What the company was actually saying was that it would rather have less qualified and able people than find a way to get a slightly bigger sized item of clothing to be worn as a uniform.

If you are wondering what the connection is between recruitment and business development, the answer is simple. It is people who deliver your services and in most cases sell your products. Get the right people and they will get the right business results. Recruit the wrong people for the wrong reasons and this will have a negative impact on the quality of everything you want to achieve.

By the way, within two years this company had crashed!

11. Keep in touch with your existing and past customers and clients

Let me ask you a question about your business. When a sale has been made or the service or job done, when are you next in touch with the customer or client? If you have just answered, *'we aren't'* or *'we don't know'*, then you are literally leaving cash on the table and you must do something about this.

There is a very simple formula to remember. The more often you communicate with your customers and clients, the more business you will get from them, their families and friends, particularly if you ask them directly for what you want. This process of ongoing communication, however, needs to be sensitive, tasteful and non-intrusive. (See Chapter 6, golden rule 3.)

12. Master social online media

The managing partner of a substantial accountancy firm told me recently, 'I'm fed up of hearing, and reading about all this social networking media nonsense. We are a serious firm with serious clients. Perhaps I'm just old-fashioned, but at our charging rates we don't have the time to indulge in computer play.'

This gentleman is certainly right about one thing … he is old-fashioned!

Let me be absolutely blunt. Regardless of size or sector, if you are not promoting yourself, your business or building relationships, using social online media such as LinkedIn, Facebook or Twitter, then you are missing out on potential business and allowing your competitors to get a differential advantage over you.

We will be taking a look later on in the book at the potential benefits of online social media opportunities for business development, with some practical tips about what you should be doing. (See Chapter 7 for more on how to use the online world for business development.)

13. Test your ideas, concepts and prices

A very dynamic, and ambitious, 'would be' entrepreneur explained to me recently how he got his fingers burnt with what he thought was a project that would make his fortune.

Because he had access to a specialised database, he decided he would send out glossy colour mailshots to all 20,000 names on the list at a price he had a positive 'gut feel' about.

Actually, he sold just nine of his products at £19 and made a huge loss on the project.

The moral of this story in business development terms is simple. He didn't test the demand for the product in the market place; he didn't test the quality of his database; he didn't test the effectiveness of his marketing copy; nor did he test his price point. Come to think of it, he didn't test anything at all or do any meaningful planning.

With big numbers lustfully rolling around in his head, he impatiently blasted out what he thought would work to his entire 20,000 database.

Had he taken his time, he could have 'split tested', sending different copy at different price points to a small but significant percentage of his database. He would have almost certainly identified whether there was a market for his product, which copy was best and at what price. Had he discovered at this stage that nobody wanted his stuff at any price at all, he could have quit before losing quite as much as he did.

Business is not, as some think, about taking wild risks. It is about making sensible and sound judgements based on information that is usually available. Test as much as you can, so you have as much information as possible.

In this way any risks you take are calculated ones, which then 'stack the odds' in your favour.

14. Plan, but keep things simple

Here is part of an introduction from a strategic business development plan. Text like this is commonly seen in the business world.

> *'The interface needs to be transformational and integrated, in order that your customers and stakeholders fully migrate towards the business re-engineering process that will be necessary, to gain full exposure and penetration of the demographic. This will trigger the internal paradigm shift, which will create greater strategic synergy across all external operational functions.'*

Wow, that's an easy one to get sorted! If any reader understood this please e-mail or call me with an explanation and translation, because I certainly don't!

All too often, plans and the planning process are dressed up to sound more complex than they need to be. Ditch the meaningless, vague, pseudo-academic business jargon and executive waffle behind plans like this, along with anyone who wants to write such stuff for you. Just keep it simple. In practice, you should know that your ability to implement a business development plan will increase in proportion to the simplicity of the plan and its language.

15. Take complaints seriously

Many years ago, I was asked to review and make recommendations for potential improvements to the complaints handling function of a large package holiday operator, which is no longer in business.

The operator had a huge customer complaints department consisting of around 70 people, processing thousands of complaints from unhappy holiday makers. Based on the corporate perception that all guests were dishonestly inventing or exaggerating problems to get some money back, every single complainant was made to feel guilty and wait for weeks and sometimes months while their complaint 'was investigated in resort'.

The most bizarre thing, however, was that the investigations consistently revealed that over 98 per cent of all complaining guests were perfectly honest and telling the truth and had justifiable cause to complain.

The overall cost of this complaints handling operation to the operator in immediate financial terms was huge and in terms of long-term damage, the cost was even greater as regards goodwill and future possible repeat business.

I'm not suggesting that complaints should not be investigated. Indeed there is a massively important quality control element to discovering what is behind customer complaints and problems. However, the operator should have dealt with the quality control element of its investigations separately from the business development objective of maintaining goodwill with its customers. Unhappy guests returning from holiday didn't need to be kept waiting months to be told that their complaint was truthful and reasonable. A presumption of honesty should have been made immediately, along with whatever apology or redress was appropriate.

The moral of this story is simple. Most customers are honest and you should do business with them on the basis of this assumption. Yes, you will get ripped off occasionally, but don't regard customers as guilty until proved innocent. It will cost you money, time and ultimately long-term damage to your goodwill.

Why is complaints handling a business development issue? Simple … if you don't handle complaints appropriately then not only do you run the risk of not getting repeat purchases, but people will stop recommending you and will tell lots of other people, not only about the initial complaint but about how badly they were dealt with. There is more on this issue in Chapter 6, golden rule 2. There you will read about how managing complaints effectively can actually boost your business.

16. Make your customer or client environment appropriate

I had a meeting recently in the lobby and reception area of a four-star hotel, part of an international chain. The décor and ambience were perfect for this business meeting but for one problem … my guest and I couldn't hear each other because of the music. It was 11 am and we were having coffee, but the music being played through the sound system would not have been out of place in a Benidorm nightclub.

I went to reception and politely asked if the music could be turned down. I was told, 'It is management policy for music to be played at this volume. It is there for the benefit of all our customers.'

Now I know I should have just left it at that, but as there were only five other customers in the same area at that time, all trying to have meetings, I actually asked them whether they would like the music to stay as it was. Guess what? All the guests wanted the music either changed, turned down or better still turned off.

I conveyed this important bit of market research to the receptionist, but it made no difference. We all still had to shout at each other for the duration of our meetings.

This is a prime example of the blatant disregard of customer opinion and preferences. I haven't been there since and I will not be going back. I suspect the other customers will avoid this hotel too for fear of going deaf!

See Chapter 6, golden rule 2 for more.

17. Train your people to spot opportunities

I recently carried out a simple and informal experiment to see whether businesses would pick up on a blatant and obvious business opportunity. I walked into three travel agents on a typical high street. Two of them were major multinationals and the other a small independent. I simply asked: 'Do you by any chance have the new Fred Olsen Cruise brochure please?' All of the agencies looked on their display shelves and said: 'We might have some in the back.' On each occasion, eventually a member of staff returned apologising for the fact that they didn't have that brochure at the moment.

Not one of them offered to take contact details so that they could let me have a brochure when they did get it in, and nobody thought behind my question and looked at me as a potential new cruise customer who might spend several thousands with them.

Despite the fact that they had glossy brochures of various other cruise lines on their shelves I was allowed to walk out of their shops without any further conversation or questions. I could have been asked, where I might want to cruise and when? It is possible that if they had found out about my preferences, they may have had something else to offer me then and there.

How many obvious and simple business opportunities do you or your colleagues miss?

18. Get out of your office or premises and mix and mingle

It is an absolute business development truth that a great deal can be achieved by fostering and building relationships. Those who find themselves permanently tucked away behind their desks and who never leave their premises will always be at a disadvantage.

Attend conferences and events, visit trade exhibitions, network with fellow business professionals and go out of your way to meet innovators, commentators and influential people and organisations dictating the pace of change. Stop and get to know and meet your competitors, build your contact base, get recognised, ask questions, make contributions, get involved in business and communal activities, and team up with other like-minded and compatible businesses and organisations for mutual support. Again, much can be achieved via social media.

See Chapter 8 on how to improve your conversational networking skills.

19. Find a niche and specialise

If you simply do what the average business in your sector does, in the average way, don't be surprised if you get decidedly average results!

It is a business development truth that you should strive to be different and one very effective way is to specialise in some way or cater for a niche aspect of your market.

Let me give you one of the best examples of this that I have seen.

> I walked past a hairdresser in Radlett, Hertfordshire. It is called 'Sharkey's Cuts for Kids' and, unsurprisingly, they specialise mainly in cutting young children's hair. Let me explain. All parents of young children know that taking little ones for a haircut can be a challenge. At this hairdresser everything is designed around creating a fun experience for children and a less stressful one for the parents. Kids can choose to have their hair cut while watching a DVD or TV, or while sitting in one of several fun chairs which include a racing car, a pink Barbie Jeep or a Mini Cooper.
>
> In gaming chairs, kids can play computer games and some of the seats are themed like a show business dressing room, complete with lights around the mirrors. The ambience is bright and colourful and appropriately themed to appeal to kids. As add-ons, they also sell appropriate merchandise, do parents' hair too, have toilets for adults and low ones for children, and have dressing-up parties.
>
> Strip away all of this packaging and the bottom line is that Sharkey's is just another hairdresser, but by making itself so different and focusing everything on one particular niche it sets itself apart and creates a unique and popular experience.

From a business point of view this is a brilliant business development example of how to get a differential advantage over other hairdressers.

The owners told me that within three weeks of opening they were very popular, with parents driving miles with their kids for hair cuts. Proprietor Sara Kahn explained, 'It is being different that makes us stand out.'

20. Model what works best

Some time ago I had a substantial client who told me, unfortunately when it was too late to help, how it had launched a television advertising campaign, marketing its 'No Win, No Fee' personal injury legal service. The client had made a major point of telling its producers to avoid what it regarded as the clichéd approach, showing people who had been injured talking about how much compensation they had received. The very 'arty' and creative but meaningless TV ad was produced at great cost, with a number of different versions, and then broadcast also at substantial cost.

The end result was that the client got only 20 enquiries from the campaign instead of the 72,000 that another organisation, which used the clichéd approach, achieved.

While of course it is a virtue to be different and to stand out, it is neverthe-less a commonsense business development truth to model what you know actually works and then adapt it in terms of strategy, in your own unique style, so that it looks and feels different.

If something has been consistently successful in the past, there is a reason for it. Don't ignore this.

21. Be squeaky clean – you need to be trusted

Some years ago, I was about to use someone for a particular business service. I had discussed a fee with him, part of which was to be payable in advance. Then I got his initial bill and an e-mail asking if I would mind if he manipulated the VAT element of the payment, so that it would in effect make it better for him and supposedly no worse for me.

I cancelled the job.

Always remember this. It is a basic business development truth that the underlying component of any business transaction is 'trust'. The moment you indicate to an existing or potential customer that you are willing to operate outside of standard ethical or legal requirements and norms, you are putting any 'trust' they may have had in you at risk.

IN SUMMARY

So to summarise then, here are the 21 commonsense business development truths again ...

1 Focus your efforts on turning your enquiries into business and not just on generating leads.

2 Exceed customer/client expectations.

3 Speak to potential customers and clients ... and speak to them nicely.

4 Be open for business when your customers or clients want to buy.

5 Don't let your administrative process become more important than doing business.

6 There's no job more important than helping customers or clients part with their cash!

7 Don't let technology get in the way of doing business.

8 Quality and word of mouth count for everything.

9 Actively strive for consistency with your quality standards.

10 Recruitment is part of business development.

11 Keep in touch with your existing and past customers and clients.

12 Master social online media.

13 Test your ideas, concepts and prices.

14 Plan – but keep the planning process simple.

15 Take complaints seriously – trust your customers or clients ... most of them will be honest.

16 Make your customer or client environment acceptable and appropriate.

17 Train your people to spot obvious business opportunities.

18 Get out of your office or premises and mix and mingle.

19 Find a niche and specialise.

20 Model what works best.

21 Be squeaky clean – you need to be trusted in business

'Great things are done by a series of small things brought together.'

Vincent Van Gogh

2

Asking the right business questions: a toolkit for business development

One of the main reasons that businesses fail to achieve their full potential and find the right answers to their business development challenges is because their decision-makers and managers simply don't ask themselves the right business questions.

I have regularly been in business development consulting situations where the questions I have asked have actually prompted management and owners to come up with business solutions for themselves. I have often seen senior people in businesses stare at each other in silence following a particular question and then in embarrassment admit, 'You don't need to say anything else ... we can see what we've missed and what we need to do.' Amazingly enough the 'killer' question that has prompted this reaction is usually something quite basic.

This chapter then is basically a list of simple, but significant, business development related questions that you can ask yourself about your venture. The intention behind them is to provoke a strong emotional reaction.

The questions are essentially a business development 'toolkit' for owners, management and directors of existing and 'start-up' enterprises. They will help you redirect your thoughts and focus. I am confident that you will find this chapter one of the most helpful and potentially powerful in the book, as the questions will trigger and inspire new ideas, act as a catalyst for action, highlight mistakes and any commercial deficiencies being made and act as a wake-up call about the important information that you should have and which is currently unavailable to you.

With all this in mind, take a look through each of the questions in this chapter, either on your own or working together with colleagues. Some of them will require a simple 'yes' or 'no' or 'don't know' response. If you answer 'no', you will need to explore why this is the case and if you respond with a 'don't know', then you will be aware of those areas where you should have more information. Other questions will require various facts and figures and yet others will require more qualitative and creative answers as you explore possible options.

Of course, not all of the questions will be relevant to all businesses. Where it is obvious that a question doesn't apply to you, simply move on. There will be very limited commentary with the questions at this stage as they are largely self-explanatory. As the book progresses, however, there will be lots of coverage about many of the areas that relate to the questions. (See the chapter/section references alongside the relevant question.)

Now let me give you the five questions that will help you make the biggest impact in the shortest time-frame. I call these the five impact questions™. They are followed by the 100 business development questions you should be seeking to answer.

The five impact questions

Here are the five general questions that will help you make the biggest impact in the shortest time-frame. Actively explore options for good answers to all these questions and then act upon them and you can be guaranteed of winning more profitable business. After these five questions, virtually everything else is mere detail.

THE FIVE IMPACT QUESTIONS

1 What **actions** do you need to take in your business to increase the conversion rate of your current leads, enquiries or opportunities into profitable customers or clients? *There is no point spending money generating more leads and enquiries until you have mastered your conversion tactics. (See Chapter 4, priority 1.)*

2 What **other** products or services do you have or can you create that you can offer or ask your existing customers and clients to buy? *(See Chapter 6, golden rule 4.)*

3   What can you do to get **existing customers and clients to spread positive word-of-mouth and tell others to buy** from you as well? *(See Chapter 6, golden rule 5.)*

4   What can you do to **increase your prices** without loss of profitable business? *(See Chapter 3.)*

5   When you have mastered your conversion of enquiries strategy and done as much as possible to develop your existing customer or client base, then **what more can you do at a sensible cost** to generate additional quality enquiries or visitors from individuals or businesses that you currently don't have as customers or clients? *(See Chapter 7.)*

Actively make time, right now, to go through each of these questions, writing down as many possibilities and options as you can come up with. Even if they seem extreme at first, get possibilities down on paper and then play with them. Bounce them off colleagues and get advice and guidance on them.

This is not the formal way to do business development or marketing planning, and many academics and purists will frown on this approach, but I can tell you as a very experienced practitioner and pragmatist … it works. Come up with effective answers to as many of these questions as you can and act upon them sensibly and you are guaranteed to experience a dramatic improvement in your business fortunes.

Just consider for a moment the effect on your business if you could:

■ convert 10 per cent more of your current leads, enquiries, visitors into business;

■ sell one additional service or product to 10 per cent of your customers or clients;

■ get 10 per cent more of them to recommend you to others;

■ increase your prices to an appropriate proportion of customers and clients;

■ generate just an extra 10 per cent more leads, enquiries or visitors.

Even if you can't manage to get these results in each of the five areas, the cumulative result from the categories you can achieve would result in exponential growth of both your turnover and bottom-line profits.

The 100 business development questions

(If a question is obviously not relevant to you, simply move on. For many of the questions, I give chapter/section references to the specific part of this book that will be most helpful.)

Converting telephone enquiries (see Chapter 5)

1   How many telephone enquiries from potential customers and clients do you get each day/week/month/year?

2   What is the average potential spend per buying customer/client per department/branch/office/shop/service?

3   What are your average conversion rates of telephone enquiries into business per branch/office/shop/department/individual?

4   What are the total telephone enquiries worth in potential revenue per week/month/year? *(Multiply the number of incoming enquiries by the average spend.)*

5   How much extra revenue would you generate if you simply converted an extra 10/20/30 per cent etc.?

6   How can you adapt your process and system so the person or people who have the best conversion rates take the majority of your calls?

7   How many of your call handlers have had proper soft skills training in techniques to get better conversion rates?

8   How do you decide, right now, who takes incoming calls? Are these geared towards getting the best conversion rates or are they simply administratively convenient?

9   How much is it costing you in financial terms at the moment to process and handle incoming telephone enquiries?

10   Is it worth considering engaging specialist sales people to deal with your incoming leads?

11   What systems do you have in place for tracking and monitoring conversion rates?

12   How easy is it to get through to your business quickly and efficiently?

13   Have you given your switchboard or reception staff appropriate interpersonal service training to deal with enquiries?

14 What active steps can you take to increase immediately your conversion rates from telephone enquiries?

15 Do the people who answer your phones know the most relevant individuals in your business to put callers through to?

16 Do the people who answer your phone know your full range of services and products?

17 What is the emotional state of your callers when they ring for the first time?

18 What do your people have to do or say to get potential customers or clients into the state that you want them in by the end of the call?

19 What do you or your people say when you're asked the 'How much?' question?

20 How do you or your team respond to 'you're too expensive'?

Dealing with visitors to your premises/shop/office

21 Are your opening hours convenient for potential customers?

22 How easy is it to find you?

23 Do you have good easy-to-follow directions?

24 What is the appearance or environment of your premises like? Will it help or be an obstacle to doing business? (*See Chapter 6.*)

25 How caring and hospitable are you to visitors coming to your shop, office or other premises? *Are they offered hospitality, do you have toilet facilities, are you child friendly etc?* (*See Chapter 6.*)

26 Do you have a proper meet and greet policy? (*See Chapter 6.*)

27 What are your toilet facilities like? (*See Chapter 6.*)

28 Do you have easy parking facilities? (*See Chapter 6.*)

29 How many visitors come to your premises per day/week/month/year to look at or talk about your goods or services?

30 What proportion of them buy from you?

31 If you have retail premises, how long do you leave visitors to browse before talking to them?

32 Do you initiate conversation or do you or your team wait for them to speak to you?

33 Do you or your people have appropriate techniques to engage a

potential customer in a conversation or are they just asked 'Need any help?'?

E-mail enquiries

34 How many people e-mail you questions about your goods and services?

35 Do you have a structured system for dealing with these?

36 To what extent do you store and use their e-mail details and information in the future? *(Subject to regulatory rules on this.)*

37 What is your conversion rate of business from e-mail enquiries?

38 What training has the person or people who deal with these had, given that this is a 'sales' role?

39 How long does it take to reply to e-mails?

General customer and client information and communications

40 How many customers and clients does your business have?

41 Can you break these numbers down per location/office/shop/ services and product range?

42 Do you have a general customer or client database? *(See Chapter 6, golden rule 1.)*

43 After they have bought from you or at the conclusion of a job, when are you next in touch with them? *(See Chapter 6, golden rule 3.)*

44 What more could you do to keep in touch with them after their initial purchase? *(See Chapter 6, golden rule 3.)*

45 Do you have up-to-date e-mail and postal addresses for your customers and clients? *(See Chapter 6, golden rule 1.)*

46 Do you have an effective IT system capable of storing and giving immediate access to customer or client information so that you can communicate with them easily?

47 To what extent do your customers and clients know the full range of your services or products? *(See Chapter 6, golden rule 4.)*

48 What percentage of customers and clients are currently returning to buy more from you?

49 How frequently are you getting recommendations and referrals via past customers and clients? (*See Chapter 6, golden rule 5.*)

50 What do you do at the moment to say 'thank you' for recommendations and introductions?

51 How much is a potential customer or client worth to you over 1, 3, 5, 10 years? (*For example, suppose you have a shoe shop selling children's shoes. You sell the parents their toddler's first pair of shoes at 14 months old. The total potential value of winning that sale is not just the £30 for the shoes, but two or three pairs of shoes per year for the child for the next 10 years as it grows. If the family has two children then it is possible that you may sell 60 pairs of shoes in total to that family. Your initial £30 sale is actually potentially worth a minimum of £1,800.*)

General marketing and business information

52 Are you able to break down your turnover into your various services or product ranges delivered or sold?

53 Who are your biggest clients and customers in revenue terms?

54 Which products or services generate the most profit?

55 Can you identify your top 10 or 20 most profitable customers and clients?

56 What do you currently do to nurture and protect your big business relationships?

57 When was the last time you spoke to your best customers or clients? (*See Chapter 6, golden rule 3.*)

58 If you were to lose one of your big clients or customers, what effect would that have on your business?

59 How strong is your 'brand'? (*See Chapter 7.*)

60 What attributes give you a differential advantage over your competition?

61 How effectively do you communicate that message to your market place?

62 What is the profile of your perfect ideal customer or client?

63 Do you have the right materials to target the right people? (*See Chapter 8.*)

64 If you are launching a new service or product, how do you know there is a demand for it?

65 If you are launching something new, how have you tested your price points?

66 When was the last time you increased your prices? (*See Chapter 3.*)

67 If you charged 10 per cent more, what would happen? How do you know? (*See Chapter 3.*)

68 What additional benefits can you offer your customers or clients to justify higher prices? (*See Chapter 3.*)

69 What has been your most successful business development or marketing activity?

70 How can you do more of what works best?

71 What product or service could become an area of specialisation for you to develop as a 'niche' business? (*See Chapter 1, truth 19.*)

72 What has been the least effective business development initiative?

73 What external things are happening in your specific sector that may create opportunities for you?

74 How can you use one or more of the social media platforms LinkedIn, Facebook, Twitter, YouTube, etc. to develop your business? (*See Chapter 7.*)

75 What are you currently doing to actively encourage positive word-of-mouth and to generate recommendations? (*See Chapter 6, golden rule 5.*)

76 How often do you mix, mingle and network at social/business events? (*See Chapter 8.*)

77 How do you or colleagues introduce yourselves when you are asked: 'So what do you do for a living?' Do you have a response that is helpful in business terms? (*See Chapter 8.*)

78 How effectively do you follow up and keep in touch with people you have met?

79 Which other businesses or organisations could you team up with for cooperation, mutual business development activities and joint ventures? (*See Chapter 7.*)

80 What are the current burning issues in your business sector that you could comment on in the media as an expert?

81 How well known are you to the local, regional or national press or trade publications, for your knowledge and expertise about your area of business?

82 How are you currently perceived by your target market?

83 Do you have a website and how effective are you at attracting relevant visitors to it? (*See Chapter 7.*)

84 Do you have genuinely helpful content and information on your site about your services or product range? (*See Chapter 7.*)

85 How effective are you at encouraging website visitors to make more direct contact with you if that is what is needed? (*See Chapter 7.*)

86 If you want customers to buy from you online, does your system inspire confidence and trust and help you build relationships? (*See Chapter 7.*)

87 How does your website help harvest visitors and build ongoing communication and relationships with prospective customers and clients? (*See Chapter 7.*)

88 If you are in the service sector, to what extent does your website influence prospective clients to want your firm or its specific individuals? (*See Chapter 7.*)

89 If you are in the service sector, where can you get speaking engagements to showcase your expertise?

90 Does your promotional material really communicate the genuine benefits of using you as opposed to a competitor, or is it simply a list of features and generic clichés?

91 If you have had to compete for business with tenders and proposals, what is your track record of success? (*See Chapter 7.*)

92 If you are failing to win the majority of these, do you know why and what you can do about it? (*See Chapter 7.*)

93 Have you ever had any proper training in the subject of winning in competitive situations? (*See Chapter 7.*)

94 What steps do you take to monitor product and service delivery quality throughout your various business premises/locations and operations? (*See Chapter 6, golden rule 2.*)

95 How do you monitor client satisfaction?

96 How do you currently use customer or client complaints as a way of enhancing and building better relationships with them? (*See Chapter 6, golden rule 2.*)

97 Are you guilty of using too much technical jargon and language about your services or products in your spoken or written communications? (*See Chapter 8.*)

98 Are you spending the majority of your business time and resources on those things that are giving you the best return? (*See Chapter 8.*)

99 What decision-making structures in your business need to be changed to ensure that the answers you have given to the questions in this chapter of the book are acted upon quickly? (*See Chapter 9.*)

100 How do you define business development success?

Finally, think of this. All the decisions that you will ever take relating to your business and the results that flow from them are actually influenced by the quality, range and frequency of the questions that you ask.

Improve your business questioning skills and you improve your business!

'The answers are all out there, we just need to ask the right question.'

Oscar Wilde

3

The 20 business development pricing tools, truths and techniques

Astonishingly, many books, articles and courses on business development don't deal with the issue of price at all. It is seen by many business writers and commentators as a completely different discipline altogether. As far as I am concerned, you can't divorce business development methods for attracting business from 'pricing' and 'charging' strategies. With this in mind, in this chapter I have created a 'mix and match' selection of ideas for you to explore, discuss, play and experiment with according to your own business type.

Some of you may think that much of what I say is basic, but are you doing it? For the rest of you, I hope that you will find it inspirational and that it could make a huge difference. How helpful the various points are will depend on: your existing general business and commercial experience; the sector you are in; the size and scale of your enterprise; whether you sell online or offline or both; whether you sell goods or services; and the stage and profile your business is currently at.

Whatever position you are in, there are a number of questions and concerns that all businesses have in common:

- What price or fee should you charge?
- Are you undercharging for some of your goods and services?
- What can you do to minimise the importance of price in the eyes of your prospects?
- What steps can you take to leverage higher prices?

- Might there be room for a total change in pricing and charging models?
- How can you get a differential advantage over your competitors through pricing?
- If you are doing something new, how do you know what price to launch at?

The 20 tools and truths in this section of the book, many of which overlap, will act as a powerful stimulus in your attempts to answer these questions.

1. Winning business is not the most important thing – being profitable is

Speaking on the subject of pricing some years ago, one of my delegates proudly boasted to a room full of people how he converted 100 per cent of his 'how much' calls into business. I asked him to share his secret.

'Oh it's easy,' he explained. 'I simply ask the caller if they have telephoned anyone else yet. If they say yes, I ask them to tell me the lowest price. Then I beat it. If they haven't rung anybody else I ask them to telephone my competitors and then come back and give me the lowest price, so that I can go even lower. This way I almost always get the job.'

Being rather curious, I asked him why, if he was so effective, he was on my course.

'Because I'm not making any money,' he confessed.

The moral of this story is simple. Too many businesses are totally driven by having a pricing or charging strategy that leads to winning the business. I have seen scores of businesses of all sizes pressured into undercutting their competitors just to get the customer or client to say 'yes'.

Over the years, I have spoken to a huge number of business people who regard it as a business virtue to be cheaper than anyone else. This thinking is totally flawed and dangerous. Price cutting is not the best weapon of choice when facing stiff competition. All that will happen is you will attract disloyal customers and clients who only want cheap, and you risk tarnishing your name and brand for ever.

Many business owners and directors will even boast about their revenue figures: 'Things are going great. We have hit the £1 million mark this year, for the first time.' That's fine providing they aren't spending around that figure to run the business. What counts is **profit**, so your ability to be able to get the maximum return is key.

Winning the business at any cost is not a great business development strategy. Do this and you risk not having a business to develop.

2. Price is a communications issue, not a financial or accounting one

While this may seem basic to many readers, I have genuinely been into many businesses where pricing was perceived essentially as an accounting and finance function. The finance people would get their calculators cranked up, work out their fixed and variable costs, add on their pre-calculated, targeted profit margins and the pricing job was done for ever. Seems straightforward, doesn't it?

While we know the lifeblood of a business is covering costs and making a profit, I want to stress that if you learn appropriate pricing and charging communication and influencing skills, and adapt some of the ideas in this chapter, your profit margins can be much, much greater than those targeted by your 'numbers' people.

3. Focus on value and service and not just price

Stop thinking for a second about your 'sales' strategy and start to think about the prospective customer or client's 'buying' strategy. Imagine that in considering whether to buy from you or not, it is as if they had a set of scales in their mind, with them consciously or unconsciously weighing up and balancing all the relevant factors.

On one side of the scales are the value and service elements and these are constantly being weighed against the other side of the scales ... the price side. This is the **value v. price scales**™.

To get good profitable prices and fees for your goods and services, what you must strive for is to pile as many 'weight blocks' onto the value and service side of the scales as possible. The more of these there are, the more they influence the prospect to actively want to buy your product or service at the price you want to charge and the more it minimises the influence and importance of price in the prospect's mind.

If you doubt this, let me ask you a question. After a purchase you have made, have you ever said to yourself or others, *'I could have got it cheaper elsewhere, but ...'* and then gone on to justify why you bought something that was actually more expensive? The 'but' reasons you give in these situations will be the 'weight blocks' of the products or services of the business you bought from and the fact that they communicated them to you effectively.

In practice, then, what do you need to consider and do in your business? Forgive the ambiguity … the answer is … get a big but!

> You must attempt to build up as many 'weight blocks' as possible before you give or present the price or discuss fees.

What this means in practice is that your ability to get a prospect to buy at the price point you want will be totally determined by your ability to communicate and pile on as many 'weight blocks' as possible. Whether your marketing and business development initiatives are on the web, in hard copy or involve face-to-face sales conversations, your overriding aim must be to get prospects into a state of such desire for the product that they are prepared to pay your price and feel good about it.

So what sort of things constitute 'weight blocks' that can create this level of desire?

Well, there isn't any one thing in particular, or even an exhaustive list. A 'weight block' can be either tangible or intangible, but ultimately it is something that will *influence* the prospect consciously or unconsciously to actively want you, your organisation or your product at the price you determine you deserve. In many cases you can assume, if they buy the same product or service from someone else cheaper, it is because you haven't piled on enough 'weight blocks' and communicated with them strongly enough to make them buy from you at your price.

The challenge for you, therefore, is to come up with and use as many 'weight blocks' that relate to your business, products or services as possible and get prospects positively lusting for your goods or services before they hear your charges.

Let me just give you a feel for a few things that might constitute possible 'weight blocks' in your business:

- your track record, experience or results – use numbers to illustrate;
- include lots of features and benefits into the price package;
- local convenience;
- testimonials or recommendations from other customers or clients;

■ impressive time factors in getting the job done or on delivery;

■ personal or business reputation;

■ quality – give examples and evidence;

■ specialisation;

■ ability to solve the customer or client's problems;

■ willingness to go 'the extra mile';

■ guarantees;

■ helpful payment methods;

■ being pleasant, polite and interested.

How many 'weight blocks' like these, or others, can you come up with relating to your products and services?

Make a list of them now with possible examples and options. How many are you currently using in your communications?

4. Bundle in and include as much as you can

How many elements can you bundle into your product for an inclusive price? How many component parts are there to your service?

The more individual elements there are and the clearer you spell these out, the greater the perceived value to the customer and the more they will be prepared to pay. Regardless of the business you are in, actively and creatively explore what you can include. There is usually something.

Let's take a trade services example to illustrate how it is possible to be innovative with 'bundling'. With apologies to any decorators who are reading this, don't just say you will paint and wallpaper someone's house and give them a price. Break down all the possible elements of your service into bullet points and find things that create the 'added value' feel. For example:

■ a no-cost home visit to measure and give a fixed quotation;

■ supply colour charts and wallpaper sample books to be left for an agreed time;

■ a book of reviews and comments from past 'happy customers';

■ free virtual design samples of rooms e-mailed to the prospect;

■ a free guide to interior design;

■ supplying of all paints and wallpapers at trade prices;

- covering all furniture and carpets service;
- preparation of all surfaces;
- removal of all old wallpaper;
- painting and wallpapering as agreed;
- end of job cleaning service;
- once a year 'decorator touch-up' service.

Decorators out there may throw up their arms in horror at all this, but actually look carefully. Many of these items are the 'norm' for decorating and some of the more creative elements are easy to provide as they are either free, or low-cost extras that you can throw in. For example, it shouldn't cost you anything to create a booklet of 'happy quotes' from past customers; your trade suppliers will give you interior design guides; and even the online design service is based on using a free web application, which even I managed to use after a minute!

How many bullet points can you come up with relating to your business? The more you can create, the more you can charge and the more desirable you become.

Be inventive. Start out by thinking what would be powerful and helpful to customers and clients.

5. Unbundle and charge things separately

Having just told you to bundle as many elements as possible into your product and service, an alternative strategy to play with is the notion of unbundling. Depending on your business and sector, you may find this will work better for you.

With unbundling, you simply work from a base price, still stacked with 'weight blocks', and sell additional items as optional paid-for extras. This way you get the benefit of potentially looking cheaper than competitors, but making additional profits by selling highly profitable 'add ons' later when they are most likely to say 'yes'. This strategy is worth considering in high-volume, very price-sensitive areas.

A good example of this concept applies to the so-called 'cheap flight air-lines'. A flight that appears cheaper to begin with can be more costly by the time you have paid for priority boarding, meals, luggage, seat choice, drinks, headsets, fees etc.

Is this a strategy you can use ethically to leverage additional business?

6. Don't fall into the price trap

One of the biggest psychological enemies of all, to you as a business, is to fall into the 'price trap'. The 'price trap' is the assumption that if someone asks 'how much?', they are only interested in 'price' and will make a decision on that alone.

Indeed, many business people on the receiving end of telephone calls or e-mails asking the 'how much?' question, all too often, actually don't hear or see it as 'how much?' but 'how cheap?'. There is a big difference and processing such enquiries in this way is a money-losing mistake.

I am not commercially naïve. Yes, I know there are some prospective customers and clients who will go to huge lengths in order to buy something a few pennies cheaper. The danger however for businesses is the automatic unconscious assumption that all customers and clients fall into this category.

Many people ask the 'how much?' question for certainty, budgetary planning and often because they simply don't know what else to ask. With this in mind, it is important to understand that whenever you are asked the 'how much?' question, it is your business development duty to attempt, where appropriate, to broaden the discussion and pile on the 'weight blocks' so that it is not totally focused on price.

Here is a provocative notion to play with. If somebody asks you for your price and you answer with nothing else but the price, it is you who is potentially forcing them to look for the cheapest.

We will be looking at techniques to deal with the 'how much?' question later in the book. (See Chapters 5 and 6.)

7. Consider increasing your prices

Some years ago I took an unusual phone call for somebody in business development. The caller said: *'We would like your help to reduce the amount of business we have. We have volume, and we are all working tremendously hard, but we aren't making enough money.'*

After a number of discussions, I simply recommended they increase their fees by between 10 per cent and 15 per cent. The result, they lost no clients, carried on working hard but generated significantly more profit.

With this story in mind, here are a few questions:

- When was the last time you increased your prices?
- What would happen if you added a small percentage or even a large percentage to your price?
- How much business would you lose to your competitors?
- How much new business might you gain from new clients who start to see you as at the premium end of your market?

Clearly it is not for me in this book to advise you to put your prices up. I'll bet you, however, that you don't have real and tested answers to all the above questions.

Time and time again, whenever I ask these questions I see business people being fearfully fixated about their prices and territorial over their often inflexible charging structures. There is always a great reluctance, particularly in a tough economic climate, to increase prices.

The thing to remember, however, is that contrary to popular perception, price is not always the only factor. If you doubt this, go for a walk up your local high street or around a nearby car park and see how many expensive cars you can spot.

When was the last time you switched your main supermarket, hairdresser, favourite food items over price? Remember, if there are sufficient 'weight blocks' people will buy from you at the prices you want.

8. Use division and comparison

Suppose you are selling an item at £450. For most people this is not a cheap casual buy. It is a substantial purchase that for many requires a considered bit of decision-making. If however you were to point out that this is the equivalent of only £1.23 per day, less than the price of a cup of coffee, your customer might look at it very differently, particularly if it was something that they could get years of pleasure and use out of. You could even go one stage further and bundle in a year's supply of coffee to add to the value and complete the business development and marketing metaphor.

How can you use this technique in your business?

9. Get others to justify your prices

Another way of making it easier to ask for and get decent profitable rates is to minimise the risks for prospective customers and clients. One of the things that holds back buying decisions, particularly expensive ones, is the 'risk' and fear of making the wrong choice. Anything you can do, therefore, to reduce the 'risk' factor increases the likelihood of someone buying from you at a good price or fee.

One of the ways of reducing risk is to provide reassurance to prospects through references or testimonials. Here are a few practical tips to help:

▥ Don't wait until a prospect asks you for a reference or written testimonial. Proactively offer this at the very beginning or make them aware that they are available.

▥ Harvest willing references and testimonials all the time. Make it part of your normal process to ask your past customers or clients if they are willing to say good things about you in writing and to get permission for you to use them publicly, for your own promotional business use.

▥ Go out of your way to ensure references and testimonials are in the public domain.

▥ Start now! Make a list of all the customers and clients you can ask for written testimonials. When they come back to you with them, make sure you say thank you and then use them.

10. Price with guarantees

As buyers and consumers of various products, we are all used to 'guarantees' and how they are used by sellers to differentiate themselves from the competition and attract our interest and custom.

For example, buy any electrical product and it will almost always come with at least a one-year guarantee or warranty hiding somewhere in the polystyrene packaging. It is a fact that guarantees have become part of the promotional platforms on which businesses compete. Indeed many leading car companies now offer a five year warranty as part of the purchase deal and at least one I am aware of has made an attempt at promoting a 'lifetime guarantee'.

If you make or sell products, build in a powerful and attractive guarantee and promote it hard.

In the service sector, however, guarantees are not offered as a matter of course. When I have suggested to some service businesses that they offer guarantees, they have looked at me as if I were an alien creature and asked: 'What can we guarantee? How can we offer refunds, we'll get ripped off?'

Despite these comments, I urge you to be bold and ask yourself, what element or aspect of your services can you guarantee? For example:

- Can I guarantee results?
- Can I guarantee time-frames?
- Can I guarantee some aspect of service delivery?
- Can I guarantee some aspect of satisfaction?

As mentioned, many people and businesses in services are hesitant to use this strategy, for fear clients will abuse the guarantee offer. In my experience this will rarely happen and even if it does, the advantages may still outweigh the disadvantages.

Be open minded and think about this rationally for a second. What are you really offering and risking? If someone were truly unhappy about your services, they would probably either refuse to pay you anyway or ask for a refund regardless of a guarantee. I am merely suggesting to you that the added attraction of a formal guarantee for some aspect of your service will not only attract more prospects and customers, but also reduces the perceived 'risk' factor inherent in every buying decision. It becomes a powerful 'weight block', which can allow you to charge a higher price.

11. Price for specialisation

This is certainly the case in the 'professional services sector'. Would you prefer to have a general surgeon or a 'cardiac specialist' carry out your heart procedure? Which would you be prepared to pay more for?

If you are in 'services' look for ways to position yourself or your firm as specialists. You should also consider the possibility of becoming niche specialists within a particular specialisation. If you are selling goods either online or in a shop, if you position and brand yourself as specialists in that sector or as having a 'specialist department', you will be able to ask and get higher prices than generic suppliers.

It will be perceived that you will, as 'specialists', have a much wider selection of goods and level of product knowledge and thus be better able to identify and match precise customer requirements.

Furthermore, even if your business is physically based miles away from your customer, many prospects may be prepared to make the journey because of the specialist nature of your business and extensive product range. For example, when was the last time you saw a specialist board game shop with both modern and vintage favourite board games in it? I saw one recently in Whitby, a small seaside resort on the north-east coast. Despite the prices being a little higher than some shops it was very busy with both casual shoppers and people who had travelled there specially because of its niche status.

12. Price for profile and experience

This is where your general business development, marketing, PR, social media networking and pricing strategies should be integrated as business partners. Although it seems obvious, there are many who provide personal or professional services who ignore this simple equation:

Profile and reputation + special experience + results = **higher prices and fees!**

Ask yourself these questions:

- How long have I been providing this service?
- How high is my profile in my sector and how well known am I and my brand?
- How many people or businesses have I helped?
- What is my track record of success, achievements, satisfaction or results?
- Am I regarded as an authority in my field?

If you rank highly on some or all the above you should be charging significantly more than someone less experienced and with a lower profile. Don't be afraid to do so and make sure in any business development initiatives or promotional copy that you include numbers and factual information on as many of the above areas as possible.

The same applies to products. Why is it that people pay many times more for Nurofen tablets than generic ibuprofen when chemically it is the same product and has the same effect? Actually, there is no one rational answer to that question. It may simply be ignorance on the part of the purchaser or in many cases it is simply down to emotional factors and powerful psychological associations. Whatever the reason, it works for the sellers and demonstrates the power of branding and being better known as a way of leveraging higher prices.

From a practical point of view, actively take steps to get your service or product range or 'brand' better known. Don't hold back ... blow your own trumpet! Some people regard it as uncomfortable or plain boastful to assert great things about themselves or their products. By all means encourage others to do this for you, but if you are waiting for this, you may have a long wait. If you don't have one, sit down now and come up with a 'trumpet blowing statement' about you, your services or products. For example:

- 'Britain's leading specialist board games retailer'
- 'The West Midlands' most experienced personal injury lawyers specialising in motor cycle accidents'.

If you have some public claim to fame ... shout about it. I recently stayed in a small, privately run guest house in Scarborough. During our short stay, the owners told me how they had recently won a Channel 4 TV programme competition for best small bed and breakfast hotel. They had press cuttings and even a 'winners' certificate about it on their wall, but were they shouting about their win as 'Channel 4 Winners' on their external promotional material and on their website? The answer is 'no'.

Be bold and tell the world about your achievements and successes and customers will happily pay more for your products and services because of it. They will even boast about it to their friends: *We paid a little more to stay in that B & B, but it was the winner of Channel 4's best small private hotel.*

13. Price based on feedback and testing

Many businesses simply make false assumptions about how much they can or can't charge based on anecdotal evidence, a minority of awkward customers and clients, fear, guilt and what the competition charges, even though competitors may not have it right either. The bottom line is that many businesses' pricing and charging strategy is based on nothing more than guesswork, with no real proper testing.

Here are a few tips and comments about price testing to consider:

- Simply asking people what they would be prepared to pay is not good price testing. Don't rely on this by itself. There is a huge difference between someone answering a hypothetical question and actually putting their hand in their pockets and parting with their money.

For example, some years ago I was chairing an international business event. In the conference room 120 delegates were asked: 'How many of you would support a new initiative costing a particular price?' Eighty-nine delegates raised their hands and a decision was taken to launch at the price mentioned. Sounds like great price testing, doesn't it. Three months later, however, the venture was launched at the voted for and 'tested' price and guess what … only seven delegates took up the deal!

The only real way to properly test your price is to offer your product for sale and see what happens. You therefore need to do just that but in a selective way before massively rolling out a new price model.

■ If possible, always look for ways to 'split test'. This is the process of offering the same product or service but at different price points and seeing what results you get. If you are offering products via mail order or over the internet it is relatively easy to do this.

Technology has made online 'split price' testing relatively simple and free of charge. In practice what happens is that visitors to your website are sent to pages showing alternative prices. This way you can assess which price pulls most orders.

Many projects when tested this way have shown surprisingly counter-intuitive results, where a higher price has outperformed a lower price.

■ With services, keep increasing your fees until you reach the price sensitivity point.

I attended a conference that addressed this issue some years ago. The speaker asked his audience of professional services providers to raise their hands if they had received complaints and negative feedback about their fees. Only three out of over 100 delegates put up their hands. With a smile on his face the presenter then said, *'Well the rest of you aren't charging' enough!'* Think about it.

If you are in services and getting an almost automatic 'yes' every time you give your fees, keep sliding them up to the point at which you start to get some resistance and hesitancy. Even be prepared to get some 'no's. If you get a 'no' this can very often still be rescued. Ultimately, you will lose far less than regularly getting 'yes' at a price that is too low.

14. Price for prestige

Why do people buy designer handbags at £599 or more from high-end designer shops when they can get a perfectly usable bag at £15.99 or less from regular high street shops?

Will the more expensive bags last a hundred times longer, hold more or be used any differently in terms of the 'junk' that is put into them? The honest and rational answer is 'no'. The same can be said for suits, cars, seats on flights, hotel rooms and a massive range of other goods and services.

Yet despite this, it is an absolute fact that you should accept, embrace and use that a percentage of people will not only be prepared to buy at the very top end but will actively go out of their way to do so ... while still seeking out the best buys and discounts at the premium end. The big question is, why? Though of course quality is a factor, it really isn't just about quality at all. Here is the honest answer and you should factor this into your pricing strategy when looking at business development.

> People don't always buy what they 'need', they buy what they 'want' and that desire is driven and fuelled by what makes them 'feel' good and gives them a sense of status and significance.

With that in mind, an important question for you to explore is: 'What is there in your product or service range that you can package and sell at the very high-end premium level?' If you don't have anything at the moment, actively sit down right now and work out what you could possibly create that fills that role. Then test by implementation until you have something that works. You will then have something that is high profitability, enhances your image, attracts loyal followers of your brand and influences others to 'want' it too.

Remember, when it comes to promoting and communicating your top end item or service, don't hold back. Potential customers will expect it to be expensive ... don't let them down!

You will need, however, to observe certain basic rules to strengthen your offering. I call this the ELVF approach. The more of these you can communicate the better:

  E = Exclusivity. Customers or clients need to feel they are getting something that perhaps others can't get. For example, I presented a big business development seminar some years ago to the legal profession. I created it as a premium priced event by allowing only one firm of lawyers from each town or city to attend. This way the justified perception from delegates was that they were getting something 'exclusive' that their competitors weren't getting.

L = Limited availability. The fewer of something there is, the more you can demand for it. This is of course similar to 'exclusivity', but it might be another peg to hang your communications on: for example, 'only two rooms left with sea views'.

V = Visibility. Most people who buy at the top end want others to know of their purchase. They may go out of their way to appear humble and modest, yet inwardly they want others to know what they have bought and can afford. This is why certain high-end products will carry highly visible and distinctive name brands on them.

F = Feel good. Make sure that any communications you use to promote and project your product or services use words that trigger the feeling and state that prospects are looking for. So words like superior, elite, exclusive, luxury, exceptional, unique, extra special, tailored, intimate, prestigious, elegant, exotic, refined, sumptuous, impeccable, supreme, meticulous, ultimate, indulgent, etc. all do the job. Get the picture? Try to sprinkle these words into your copy, along with congruent 'feel good' images.

15. Price for know how

Have you heard this story?

A man was driving home one evening when his car broke down. A passing mechanic stopped and offered to try to get the car going again for a modest fee. After gazing at the engine for 30 seconds the mechanic then banged once on the body of the car with his fist. He then invited the owner to get in and start it up. Amazingly it started first time.

'Fantastic,' the owner said. 'How much do I owe you?'

'£25,' said the mechanic.

'£25 for one bang on the bonnet … that's just ridiculous,' said the man.

'No,' replied the mechanic, 'for the bang on the bonnet I only charged £1, but for knowing where to bang, I charged £24!'

Remember, however long the job takes, the real value your client gets is that you know where to bang. If you are in services, make sure you charge appropriately for this.

16. Price with the competition in mind

This concept is particularly relevant to those in the services sector and is something I stumbled across almost accidentally after a very large number of 'mystery shopper' research projects.

If you were to look at and research your immediate and direct competitors as regards fees in any town, city or local market place you would typically find one or two firms or businesses which were significantly cheaper than the rest and maybe one or even two which were massively more expensive. The rest however would fall into what I call the 'middle ground' and predominately this is where the battle over price is being fought and where the majority of people will buy.

What is most significant, however, is that if you look at the comparative fees at the top and bottom ends of the middle ground you will find the difference in charging rates is almost always relatively small. With this in mind, consider positioning yourself immediately at the top end of the middle ground. If you are able to develop good enquiry handling techniques and pile on the 'weight blocks', any small fee difference should not work against you. (See Chapter 5.)

17. If you must have a loss leader, make it count!

Many businesses internally justify their low prices and fees as a loss leader, their reasoning being that they will attract interest, potentially win some business and enable you to generate a bigger spend either then or in the future.

While the logic of the loss-leader concept is absolutely fine and in many cases very successful, I have also seen it work against businesses. With this in mind, plan carefully how you are going to make your 'loss leader' work for you in the future. If part of the plan is to use it to build relationships with customers and clients for the future, then you must have in place a programme for keeping in touch with them and nurturing that relationship.

Remember, if you don't get them to come back or sell them something else at profitable levels, it is not a loss leader, it is just a loss!

18. Consider special deals, promotions, sales and discounts

Read any daily newspaper any day and you will find it littered with huge numbers of advertisements based almost entirely around special deals, discounts and percentage savings. The same can be said if you walk down any high street, through any shopping centre or supermarket.

Why is this? Are we a nation of bargain hunters always looking for a good deal? The simple answer is 'yes', everyone likes to get a good price and always remember that nobody is above the attraction of a 'special offer'. I have met, mixed with and worked with some very wealthy business people and leading entrepreneurs and without question they know how to watch what they buy and to negotiate hard. They might buy at the top of the range but they will still want to know and feel they have got a great deal.

With this in mind, whatever business sector you are in, whether you are selling goods or services, don't ignore the importance and possibility of using 'special deals' as a way of attracting new business.

This is a huge topic, way too big for detailed attention in this book, but to stimulate your thinking and prompt some internal discussion, here are a few ways you can offer, package and pitch your 'price'-related offers. Which of these you use, if any, will depend on your type of business, your sector, seasonal issues and current market and economic trends.

While many of the following will be very familiar to you, in many cases they will be associated with particular market sectors. Be creative and look at each of them to explore how they can be adapted, if at all, in concept to your business:

- *Focus on percentage discounts*: for example, 'Up to 50 per cent off marked prices.'
- *Focus on savings*: for example, 'Save £200 per couple on next year's holiday.' Instead of talking about a vague percentage reduction, you actually quantify precisely 'how much' your customers or clients will save on a particular purchase.
- *More product or service for the price*. This is the famous BOGOF – 'buy one, get one free' – concept or the notion of offering customers or clients extra in some way. How effective are these? Well, research indicates they can be very successful, particularly as a technique for getting consumers of commodity items to try different brands. I have

seen research that indicates that as many as 87 per cent of consumers would switch from their usual brand in response to a sudden BOGOF promotion. The big question, however, is whether they would switch back when the promotion ends.

■ *Focus on a deal towards particular target customers*: for example, when my kids were little and we were on holiday, we always looked out for those 'free kids' meals with each adult meal purchased' offers. Not only did they attract our custom, but by cleverly limiting the available menu choices of both child and adult meals, the business owners could still do very well.

Here are some additional practical tips with special deals:

■ *Create extra leverage by making any offers you have time sensitive and/or limited by numbers available.* Tempting your prospects with a great money-saving deal will, in many cases, be attractive enough to make them look and be tempted. Telling them, however, that the 'deal' ends on a specific date creates additional urgency and real leverage to buy. Having limited stock or numbers available also makes it even harder to walk away. For example, 'Offer must end midnight tonight' or 'Only five rooms left'.

■ *Keep it clean and ethical.* If you say your 'sale or special deal ends today', stick to it. If you simply have another sale next week, or keep extending it, the power of leverage is lost. You also lose credibility and trust. If you lie about that, people wonder what else you might cut corners on.

Note there are strict rules about how you advertise 'sales' and 'special reductions' so check them out first. There are businesses out there which manipulate them to their advantage while technically not being in breach of the law. The big question, however, is, do you really want to develop a business that way and how many customers/clients will want to stay loyal to you if you do?

19. Price for easy payment

When giving serious thought to your pricing and charging strategy, remember also to give major consideration to how people pay. There may be organisations or people who would like to buy from you but have difficulty in terms of immediate affordability.

With this in mind it is important to factor into your charging strategy ways of making it easier to pay. If you can do this then it will be a powerful influence on getting the price you want.

At its simplest level setting up a facility for customers to pay by credit cards may help. Somewhat more sophisticated are deals we have all seen such as 'Pay nothing for 12 months, then pay over 48 months, 0 per cent interest'. This is hugely attractive and appears to many as a very painless way to buy. The fact that the bottom line price might in some situations actually be higher to allow for this deal will somehow get lost in the promotional translation, particularly if it is wrapped up at the outset as a 'discounted sale deal'.

The important question for you then is this: what can you do to ease the burden of paying? In some situations, the easier you can make it, the more you will sell at the price or fee you want.

20. Price with magic numbers

Which of these prices will attract more buyers: £19.99 or £20? The answer will almost always be £19.99. Is it because we are 'cheap-skates' at heart and want to save the penny? In most cases we know rationally that this doesn't really make any huge financial difference in terms of savings, but our psychological and emotional response to it is different. It 'feels' lower as the first figure mentioned is lower. This is really bizarre as we know it is an illusion, yet we are continually sucked into it. We even use it ourselves, when telling and justifying to friends and family members how much we have paid for something. We tell them ' ... *and I got the new car for under £10,000'*, when actually we paid £9,995 for it! This is a simple trick. Is it something you can use?

There is also an urban myth, that I must add I have absolutely no direct research or opinion on, that a price figure ending in a '7' gets good results and a '3' is to be avoided. The best way to find out is to test it. If you come up with something significant, do let me know.

'There is scarcely anything in the world that some man cannot make a little worse, and sell a little more cheaply. The person who buys on price alone is this man's lawful prey.'

John Ruskin

4

Introducing the business development priorities

One of the questions that I am asked more than anything else when it comes to business development is ... where do we start? The truth is that most businesses start at the wrong end. Many begin by throwing most of their business development resources at various costly activities and initiatives, either online or offline, to generate leads and enquiries. Indeed many readers of this book will have bought it in the hope that it might stimulate some great new 'lead generation' ideas. Well ... the good news is that it will, but the even better news is that there are other priorities to focus on first, which are usually easier, cheaper, more controllable and, here is the best bit ... if done properly, will produce instantly dramatic results and higher profits for you. Interested?

Understanding these priorities – there are three of them – the **business development priorities**, is your key to unlocking your 'missing millions'. Yes, I mean it quite literally, the majority of businesses are under-achieving and actually losing business that they could win, simply because they are not starting in the right place and not getting their priorities right.

So now we'll look at the correct business development priorities for you, which will provide the foundation for much of the rest of the book and your future business development strategy, thinking and success.

You should focus your attention and resources on these three priorities in the order they are mentioned. I will then explain a little more about each of them so that you understand why this bit of business philosophy is so important. As the book progresses I will also give you the techniques, structures, tools and know how for each one of them.

The business development priorities

Priority 1 – Convert existing leads, opportunities and enquiries into profitable business

Priority 2 – Develop more business from existing customers and clients

Priority 3 – Externalise business development efforts to generate new leads, opportunities and enquiries

---

You will notice here a complete reversal of what most businesses actually do in practice. Going flat out to produce new enquiries and leads is actually only third on my priority list. Let me explain why, by looking at each of them in turn.

Priority 1 – Convert leads, opportunities and enquiries into profitable business

There are endless courses, articles and high-tech, high-priced programmes giving you 'really cool' ways of massively generating more leads. Every time I check my e-mails, I can guarantee that some 'guru' somewhere has sent me a pitch about their 'unique' system. Here are the irresistible messages from one sample day:

- '7 Steps To Jump Start Your Promotion And Get More Leads'
- 'Boosting Your Lead Generation'
- 'How To Triple Your Leads'.

Do any of these look familiar? To be fair, lead generation *is* vital and many of these messages may genuinely offer you solid material, which really works if implemented properly. *But* I have yet to receive a single piece of communication that helps readers or delegates make the ultimate connection between generating the leads and turning them into business. One without the other is like a football team creating lots of goal-scoring opportunities without the know how, ability or even recognising the importance of putting the ball in the back of the net and scoring!

Contrary to the internet hype about this, leads by themselves will *not* make your business prosperous and profitable. This comes only when you have taken that opportunity and converted it into business at the best possible price.

The key bit of logic then is this:

> What is the point of spending time, money, creative energy and manpower on generating leads and business opportunities if you don't convert as many of them as possible into business at the most profitable levels?

Let me repeat this because it is so fundamentally important. If your external business development initiatives are successful, they will not produce business. They will merely bring you leads and enquiries, which still have to be converted, and that is a different process and skill. These leads might come in by phone, visitors walking in, via e-mail or website traffic. However they turn up, picture that lead, enquiry or opportunity as a potential amount of money and revenue dropping into your 'enquiries bucket'.

Because many businesses haven't made the processing of these leads a priority, by investing in analysis, tracking, developing a proper structure and appropriate staff training, a percentage of these leads fail to become business at all. Putting it another way, many of these business opportunities are simply leaking away through a small or even big hole in the bottom of the 'enquiries bucket'!

Do you know how most businesses respond to this? They simply perceive that they don't have as much business as they would like, so go out and spend more cash on more external business development activities to produce more leads. Guess what happens to them. Exactly … many of them continue to leak away through the same hole in the leaky bucket. With this in mind, let me ask you: do you have a leaky 'enquiries bucket'? How much business are you losing that you could win?

With all this in mind, Priority 1 is about plugging the hole in the bucket. See the next chapter for a strategy and set of techniques for mastering this priority.

Just to illustrate the point in cash terms:

> I was invited to train and coach a substantial household brand name business, that admitted it could see the logic of what I was saying and would like to explore this re-thinking of priorities with me.
>
> They told me that for one of their services and products, they received 4,800 enquiries a year by telephone, with an average spend of £1,250. I got them to appreciate that, taken collectively, these leads, brought about through their various efforts, were worth a potential £6 million per year, being fed into their 'enquiries bucket'. Their conversion rate they told me, when pressed and analysed, was 43 per cent. Thus the majority of their leads, a substantial chunk of possible business, was leaking away.

By re-focusing their efforts, making this issue a priority, understanding exactly what was happening and giving relevant staff appropriate training and simple techniques, the conversion rate increased by 25 per cent in less than three months. On average then, as a result of them re-defining their priorities, this process was worth an extra £1.5 million per year.

It also meant that there were a lot more individuals coming into their customer base who might buy other services and products from them. (See Priority 2.)

Now, I know there will be some cynics reading this who will say that converting enquiries is not the number one issue to start with for them. Some may argue that as a new business they don't have any enquiries or leads at all to worry about and thus getting leads is where they should be putting their major focus. I completely understand this argument, but it is short sighted, as the same logic applies. Why would you want to invest in getting leads until you know you have an effective and practical plan in place for converting as many as possible at the best prices, as and when they *do* come in?

The other argument I hear is this. Given the current economic climate many business people have said to me that as there are fewer enquiries around in many sectors, their focus should be on promotional activities to generate as many new leads as possible. Again, this seems to have some intellectual merit. However, in my opinion it is still flawed. It is precisely because there may well be fewer enquiries and leads around that you need to make sure that you're doing the maximum and not the minimum to turn as many of them as possible into income and profit.

It is a fact that the past few years have been tough in many areas of business. You may not personally be able to influence the economic climate in your favour, but the one thing you can control is the way in which you process and manage your existing opportunities and enquiries to maximise your conversion rate. If there are fewer enquiries around, then every lead that you allow to leak through your 'enquiries bucket' is likely to be harvested and converted by a competitor who deals with enquiries better than you.

By the way, I have come across many businesses which don't need to do anything but focus on improving their conversion rates to make a dramatic difference to their bottom line. It is the one area where every business can make an instant guaranteed difference.

Priority 2 – Develop more business from existing customers and clients

Your second business development priority should be about leveraging more business from your existing customers and clients. Let me give you several important reasons why this takes precedence over Priority 3, which is all about new lead generation.

Loyalty leading to repeat purchases

It is easier to get existing clients to make repeat purchases from you than to get businesses or people who don't know you at all to switch brands or loyalty. When, for example, did you as an individual last change your brand of coffee, washing powder, baked beans, hairdresser, plumber or supermarket? As a business how long is it since you considered trying a different accountant, bank or solicitor? Most customers and clients are resistant to change so long as they are happy with a particular service, product or person.

Potential to sell other products, services and extras

If you have or can create additional items, extras or something new to launch, your existing base will be easier to get at and more likely to be receptive to other related products or services. Depending on the strength of your brand, sometimes potential customers will even be desperate to buy from you. If you doubt this, just look at the queues of Apple fans outside Apple Stores when a new iPad, iPhone or other 'must have' Apple 'iGizmo' comes out. Not only are these people driven to buy the latest gadget, but they will also spend even more cash on a new case and other related accessories.

Inside knowledge of customer or client

With some smart gathering of information, your inside knowledge of the customer or client makes it easier to proactively target other relevant goods or services at them, that your competitors won't know are appropriate. For example, if you have bought this book from Amazon, it will know and interpret your buying habits and intuitively e-mail you with other titles 'that you may like'. In the services sector, a solicitor who has just handled a divorce for you will know that you are in the market for a new will and if they are clever, get to you first.

Cheaper and less speculative

I can pretty much guarantee that whatever external business development activity you engage in, it will be more expensive and speculative than tapping into your existing base. Thus by focusing on existing customers and clients first, you can generate easier business for less cost, leaving you with additional cash to put into external lead generation activities to feed your 'enquiries bucket' at the appropriate time.

You can often charge higher prices

Generally speaking, with your existing contact base, the price you can charge will be easier to increase or maintain as you will have an existing relationship with customers based on loyalty to your service, product range or brand. Whether it is justified or not, you may feel more price pressure from new and totally cold enquiries. (See Chapter 3 on pricing.)

Positive word-of-mouth

Developing your existing customer and client base is also like recruiting an informal 'sales team'. Look after customers and they will become advocates for you, spreading positive word-of-mouth to their friends, colleagues and relatives. Any purchases they make from you is business that you have not had to buy through external business development activities.

When you look at this list of benefits, it is an absolute business development anomaly that most businesses spend the biggest part of their budget and resources on Priority 3 ... generating new enquiries. If this is you, regardless of your size or sector, it is time to have a huge re-think.

> I am not telling you to give up on external lead generation activities, they are of course vital. I am however urging you to focus on Priorities 1 and 2 first.

In Chapter 6 I will give you the five golden rules of generating more business from your existing base and many tools, techniques and tips to help you make them work in practice. You will of course then need to choose which ones you find most useful and adapt them as appropriate.

Priority 3 – Externalise business development efforts to generate new leads, opportunities and enquiries

Now I know that some of you will want to jump straight to the chapter on this, but be strong. Resist the temptation to flick forward in this book, as your focus should be entirely on Priorities 1 and 2 first and you should only contemplate serious action in Priority 3 *after* you have worked out what you are going to do about the first two areas and have taken decisive action to progress them.

With this note of caution in mind, the third priority is about exploring a wide range of external offline and online business development activities. I will set out some tried and tested methods for you to select from and give you straightforward tips on how to put them into practice in a way that actually gets results. To be specific, I will be looking at the internet and social media networking, joint venture collaborations, competitive pitching, branding and direct telesales.

5

Priority 1 – Convert leads, opportunities and enquiries into profitable business

If you are easily converting 100 per cent of your leads and enquiries into business at the prices that you really want and are totally satisfied that improvement is impossible, then you can skip this chapter and write to me with your secret. Perhaps we'll publish it together! If, however, you are not getting the results that you would like and want to explore a relatively quick, inexpensive and almost guaranteed way to develop your business, then read on.

In case you are one of those people, sitting there, book in hand, thinking to yourself, 'I think we're pretty good at this conversion issue,' let me spell out again why this topic is the place to start your business development.

As an informal bit of research, I recently telephoned 20 businesses in various sectors as a potential customer or client, with a general query about their various products, services and prices. Here is a depressingly blunt summary of some of my experiences and what I encountered:

- At four businesses nobody was available to speak to me, and only two offered a call back.
- Neither of the two which had offered to call me back actually called.
- At two organisations, I never got past reception or switchboard. They simply gave me a price and terminated the call.
- At five businesses, I was put through to the wrong person … someone who couldn't help at all.

- I was told by one service business, 'We don't give figures over the phone.' End of call!
- At one professional practice firm I was told, without any prompting, 'I can give you a figure, but we don't do cheap!'
- In only three calls did anybody engage me in a real and proper conversation and ask about my requirements.
- Only twice was I asked what had prompted my call to them.
- Not one business gave me any specific reasons why I should choose them as opposed to a competitor.
- Only three offered any written follow-up information but **only one** actually kept its promise and sent me anything.
- Not one organisation asked if I would like to go ahead and do business with them.
- Fifteen out of the 20 made me feel like I was a nuisance, and that they would be doing me a favour by dealing with me.
- In three of the calls I was on telephone hold for over two minutes.
- In a third of all calls neither party to the call knew who they were talking to. In other words, they hadn't asked my name nor did they give theirs.
- In only four calls were any contact details asked for.

Just to give you a slightly better feel for how some of my actual conversations went, one of my calls triggered this short dialogue with someone on reception/switchboard, who had already told me to call back later and ask for a specific person. I did call back at 11.15 in the morning and here is the conversation:

Me: Hi, I wonder if I can speak to Mr Smith please ... I called earlier. *(Name changed to protect the guilty.)*

Switchboard: I'm sorry, he's just popped out for a haircut and then he's going straight to lunch ... he always likes to take his lunch early.

Me: Okay, what time will he be back?

Switchboard: Well he is often late back. He likes long lunches, I'd leave it until after 3 pm, if I were you ... but don't leave it too late as he often goes home early ... he likes to play golf you see!

Now there's a man who knows about the 'work/life balance'!

By the way, these results are not exceptional. I have, over the years, made hundreds of similar mystery calls ... I have even made some of them live from my public seminars in front of large audiences ... and encountered these sorts of responses as standard. Bear in mind, too, that all the businesses telephoned in the survey above spend serious money trying to generate just the kind of calls I made. All of them have a 'leaky enquiries bucket', but most won't be aware of it.

Let me ask again … how much business are you losing?

As a commercial trend, at first sight this may seem rather negative and disturbing, but as someone with an interest in business development, you should see this very opportunistically. The enlightened readers among you should have worked out by now that this generic 'equality of inefficiency' gives you and your business a great opportunity to stand out and 'clean up' in your sector, if you can get it right.

For any cynics among you, let me give you a taste of the kind of average results you can achieve. Businesses which review their processes for dealing with enquiries and properly adopt the strategies and methods I am about to set out typically see an increase in success rates of around 10 per cent within the first month and many triple their conversion rates within six months. By the way, I have also seen businesses that have dramatically increased conversion rates also increase their prices at the same time. More conversions at higher prices … imagine what effect that would have in your operation!

So what are these magic strategies and techniques? What exactly do you need to do in your business to improve and increase your conversion rates? Well, the good news is that they are all very basic and straightforward. In fact, they are so obvious that they are all too often overlooked.

I set out below the general concepts first, my **10 commandments of converting leads and enquiries.** Only when you have understood and processed these will you be totally ready to adopt my **five-step conversion process** with total confidence and commitment.

Everything I'm going to tell you applies equally to leads and enquiries being dealt with over the telephone (incoming or outgoing call backs) or through face-to-face visitors to your premises.

I will, however, give you a few additional tips on dealing with e-mail enquiries later and in Chapter 7 on the internet and social media I will specifically be examining the issue of converting website traffic into business.

The 10 commandments of converting leads and enquiries

The 10 commandments

1 Understand that everyone who talks to prospects is in 'sales'.
2 Challenge and question current methods and results.
3 Quantify the potential revenue from leads and enquiries.
4 Track and monitor the right information.
5 Get the batting order right.
6 Differentiate – understand the test drive concept and that 'feelings' are everything.
7 Don't fall into the price trap.
8 Get the basics of telephone first response and meet and greet right.
9 Get outside help – ACT.
10 Understand and master the five-step conversion process.

1. Understand that everyone who talks to prospects is in 'sales'

When it comes to dealing with leads and enquiries it is vital for you, your call handlers or whoever physically meets customer prospects to understand that they have a 'sales' role. This might seem like a statement of the obvious, but all too often, callers and visitors are simply 'processed' as a matter of administration and in many cases the prospective customer or client is almost made to feel like a nuisance. Thus I want you to start thinking of your customer service team, receptionists, assistants, support staff, administrators, switchboard people, in fact anyone who might have contact with a prospect, as in 'sales'. Yes, I know many 'job descriptions' might not mention this, but let me explain why all these people do have a 'sales' role.

The fact is that anyone who contacts your company with an enquiry is in a buying position. Whether they have telephoned with a question about price, or walked into your shop or premises to ask about a product or just to get a brochure, they have the power and choice to buy from you, someone else, or not at all.

Therefore, if they are a potential buyer and someone from your company is dealing with their enquiry, then as a matter of logic, your colleague, whoever they are, is occupying a sales role, whether they like it or not.

This being the case, they need to know it, be comfortable with that fact and become good at influencing prospects to actively want to do business with your organisation.

2. Challenge and question current methods and results

One of the most common problems I find in businesses of all sizes is that they rarely just take time out to stop, look at existing methods of dealing with leads and enquiries, challenge what they are doing and look at conversion results strategically. In fact, many fail to have any proper conversion tracking information at all to work from.

In many businesses, methods for dealing with the leads and enquiries have simply evolved organically. I often find that team members 'do their own thing' with little effective training or analysis. Many dealing with telephone leads are on mental auto-pilot, so that every caller or visitor is dealt with in virtually the same way. So, for example, the telephone goes and the call handler's brain automatically flips into 'call handling mode' and out come the same questions, same information and all delivered in the same tone of voice. Now this would be fine if it got great results at the most profitable rates on a sustained basis. The problem, however, is that this is not always the case.

Thus, the second commandment is to accept as a matter of business philosophy the need to stand back and strategically analyse the current picture.

3. Quantify the potential revenue from leads and enquiries

Understanding just how much is at stake creates leverage for change. Once you know just how much even a small increase in conversion rates is worth to your business it adds power and influence to your efforts and justifies the time, resources and often mental shift required by personnel to adapt to new methods.

So one of the first things you need to do, to demonstrate to yourself or colleagues just how phenomenally important this area is, is to actually sit down with a calculator, spreadsheet or pen and paper and quantify with a reasonably acceptable degree of accuracy the potential revenue from your existing enquiries and leads.

Let's suppose then that an average customer spend is £1,000 and you average four enquiries a day in each five-day week. This means you're generating at the moment 20 enquiries a week. To keep the maths simple, let's assume 50 working weeks in the year. This means then that you are dealing with 1,000 leads in the year, at an average revenue of £1,000 per enquiry. This represents £1 million a year.

Without any external spend on business development activities, promotion or marketing, if you are able to increase your conversion rate of purchases off these leads by 20 per cent this is worth an extra £200,000 to you. That of course doesn't factor in the number of extra customers and clients who will buy other goods and services from you again in the future.

Obviously you will need to do your own calculations based on the number of leads you generate and of course the financial value of your various products and services. However, the simple formula always remains the same:

> Number of leads/enquiries for specific goods or services × the average customer or client spend on them = potential revenue.

Have you ever worked this out?

4. Track and monitor the right information

Given the above commandments about quantifying the potential and questioning your current methods, it should be obvious to you now that it is vital for you to have reasonably precise statistical tracking information on the enquiries and leads that are being generated and your current conversion rates.

Here are the basic items of information that you should have in order to be able to track and monitor this area effectively. If you don't have this information then you are trading and operating at a business disadvantage and if you really want to improve your business development results then you need to take steps to fill this gap in your strategic knowledge.

- How many new enquiries do you get per day/week? *(If you can do this exercise for different products or services and locations, so much the better.)*
- What are your leads and enquiries worth in average revenue terms?
- Who actually handles the enquiries and has 'conversion responsibility'?
- What are their personal conversion rates?

Once you have this information, you will be in a much stronger position to make decisions about new strategies, structures and techniques and of course to measure future improvements.

How you record and track this information will vary of course from business to business according to its size, sector and scale of operation. Small businesses may be able to do it manually, while bigger enterprises may devise and create their own software applications to perform this task.

However you do it, one very practical tip: *keep it as simple as possible.* Go for the minimum of information as mentioned above that will be helpful and track it well, rather than trying to gather too much information and ending up doing it badly.

5. Get the batting order right

Understand this concept and implement the suggestions and I absolutely guarantee an increase in your conversion rates, even if you do nothing else at all.

Let me explain: just as in a game of cricket where it is generally accepted that the best batsmen go in to bat first, you need to make sure that those enquiry handlers in your organisation who currently get the best conversion rates handle the most prospects.

So for example, with telephone enquiries, the reality for many small and medium-sized organisations is that it is almost random who handles incoming telephone enquiries from prospects. One of the first questions I ask business development people is: what determines who actually handles incoming new business calls? Here is a sample of the most common responses I get:

- 'We have a rota so that no one person gets too burdened down with dealing with telephone enquiries and leads.'
- 'Bob deals with enquiries on Monday, Wednesday and Friday afternoons and Sally deals with them on Tuesday, Thursday and Friday morning.'
- 'We pass all enquiries through to whoever is least busy.'
- 'If it's just the price someone wants, switchboard have the figures … they can give them out.'
- 'We don't want the senior staff wasting their time talking to callers, so we have their secretaries deal with them.'

With the Bob and Sally example, this sort of administrative-led process is fine assuming that both Bob and Sally get broadly similar results in terms of the conversion rates. However, what if Bob gets three times better results?

Surely as a matter of commercial commonsense it is ludicrous for Sally to handle as many of the leads as Bob. At the very least get Sally some training to help her improve how she handles leads.

My recommendation and strategy are incredibly simple and dramatically effective. Monitor, track and find out who gets the best conversion rates and then do whatever you have to do to make sure that that person handles the majority of enquiries.

Provided you have managed this process sensitively within your organisation, it is inevitable that your overall average conversion rate goes up and thus your revenue and profits are increased.

6. Differentiate – understand the test drive concept and that 'feelings' are everything

Have you asked yourself this very blunt question? Why should a potential customer or client choose my product or service as opposed to a competitor's? Ultimately what is it that is going to differentiate you and your business from the competition?

I'll tell you what the most common answers are when I ask businesses this question:

- 'We are friendly and approachable.'
- 'Because we give a quality personal service.'
- 'We sell reliable quality products.'
- 'We are efficient.'
- 'We are a specialist business.'
- 'We like to take an interest in our customers and clients.'

I have been given these sorts of responses thousands of times. The list of meaningless platitudes is almost endless. Yes, I did say meaningless and I'll tell you why. In most cases these are not points that distinguish you from your competition, they are simply implied attributes of all people in business who have goods or services to sell. Virtually everyone says the same few things.

By the way, if you are finding it hard to come up with something that absolutely differentiates you from your competitors, think how much harder it is for a prospective client or customer, who doesn't know your business at all, to appreciate why they should go with you.

The really important thing is not necessarily what you say, but how you make the potential customer or client feel. Think of the enquiry call or visit to your premises as a 'test drive'. If you haven't dealt with them before then the whole experience and encounter is for them as if they were 'test driving your business', insofar as they have the chance to experience what you are like.

Thus what is of paramount importance is that they are respectfully and courteously dealt with in a way that reflects the fact that you are interested in them and genuinely appear to want their business. The old adage of 'people buy people first' is absolutely true in this situation. If a prospective customer doesn't like the individual they are dealing with at your company, it will make it that much harder for them to make a happy and positive buying decision in your favour.

If you doubt this, just for a moment, stop and think of a situation when you have been on the telephone or face to face with somebody talking to you about their services, goods and prices and you have had to decide whether to buy from them or someone else. Have you ever had that moment when you are in the middle of one of these buying conversations when a little voice in your head whispers, *'There's no way I am buying from them'*? What was it that made you feel like that? Was it something they said? What was it that brought on this negative reaction? I have asked many people this question and the most common response is usually, *'I don't really know … it was just a feeling.'*

What about the opposite? Have you ever been in a buying or decision-making situation and instead of the negative whisper, you have felt a positive tingle or shiver up your spine as this time the voice in your brain goes *'Yes, I quite like them.'* Again, what was it that brought about this response? What did they say or do that triggered such a positive reaction? The most common response is again the same, *'I really don't know, it was just a feeling.'*

Callers or visitors to your company making a potential business enquiry will, at some point in the process, hear that little voice in their head and experience this 'just a feeling' moment. Whether it is a negative one or a positive one is absolutely determined by the way in which the enquiry handler deals with the prospect, but rest assured the outcome of that 'feeling' will play a huge part in whether you convert the business or not at the price you want.

7. Don't fall into the price trap

As mentioned in the section on pricing, the price trap is the automatic assumption that everybody who pops into your premises or calls and asks for the price will only ever choose the cheapest. This is simply not the case. If that is your perception and experience then I invite you to consider that this is largely because you are either not doing anything else other than giving a price, or you are generally not handling the enquiry as well as you could. If you only give the price to those who ask, then it is you who reduces the issue to one of price and you who actually forces them to go to the cheapest.

To prove the point, I have often had the opportunity of monitoring conversion rates for a number of different businesses. There is a huge discrepancy in conversion rates between different people within the same organisation trying to sell the same products or services, despite the fact that they are all working to the same prices or fee levels. If their respective conversion rates based on the enquiries that they deal with are A 18 per cent, B 43 per cent, C 31 per cent, and D 76 per cent, how do you explain the difference in results if all of them are working to the same price or fee structure? It is clearly not about 'price', it is more to do with technique and performance. That is what we will look at shortly.

8. Get the basics of telephone first response and meet and greet right

So far as telephone enquiries are concerned, it's worth remembering that by the time your call handlers actually speak to a prospect, they may well have already gone through a switchboard or reception process and formed potentially irrevocable impressions of your business. With this in mind you really need to go back to the basics of making sure that the people who are your first response operate to a set of high standards. Remember, if you don't tell them precisely how you want your calls to be answered, then don't be surprised if they do their own thing.

I could fill a whole chapter on how switchboard or reception staff should deal with incoming calls but the basic objectives should be to:

- pass the caller through to someone who can help as fast as possible;
- take the name of the person calling and tell them who they're going to be put through to;
- give the call handler the name of the person they have on the line;
- apologise to the caller if there is a delay;
- take the prospect's number, name and brief details if the relevant person is not available and arrange when it is convenient for a call back. If at all possible, it is always better to have the call dealt with

first time around. If it gets left, then the prospect may have done a deal elsewhere by the time someone gets back to them;

■ avoid inappropriate excuses about why certain people are not available. For example, I have had switchboard staff say to me, *'I can't put you through to Mr Smith at the moment because he's just gone to the toilet so he might be a while'*;

■ deal with the caller with an interested, courteous, helpful, warm and friendly tone. Some communications experts talk of 'putting a smile in your voice'. I'm not sure I would personally use that phrase, but it gets the message across.

One of the great irritants of our technological and digital age is the 'call centre' hold or the 'menu selection' system. You know the routine, *'for sales press one, for accounts press two, to speak to a human being press three'*.

It is a curious fact of modern life that these systems are universally hated by almost everyone. Have you ever encountered somebody who says, *'Hey those phone menu systems are great ... I really like listening to them'*? Yet the same people who despise them, when they are making calls, suddenly decide they would be great to install in their own businesses.

I am prepared to accept that they might make sense in large organisations with huge call volumes that are able to deal with incoming calls more inexpensively by having them dealt with by call centres. However, it is time for some business development 'tough love'. Your potential customers and clients don't like them and it is not helping your cause.

It is actually very simple: the more you distance yourself from your prospects and the more barriers you erect in the contact process, the less likely prospects will be to buy from you. In short, then, if you can avoid these devices, do so.

The same applies to your front line 'meet and greet' people. If prospects visit your premises or shop and are not dealt with properly, then you are potentially losing business and you may never know about it.

9. Get outside help – ACT

If you want to get dramatic results, then you must understand this acronym ... ACT.

A = Analyse. Ideally you need someone from outside, taking a hard and critical look in, as if they were a prospect. They should be looking at your available 'conversion' information, making mystery calls and visits to find out what is really going wrong and where the 'leak' is in your 'enquiries bucket'.

C = Create new system. As a result of the analysis and mystery checks, a tailored new system, structure and method of handling enquiries should be created to rectify the weaknesses found.

T = Training. This then needs to be carried out to implement the new system. It should include:

- information and presentations to relevant team members to get them to understand the nature of the problem, the concepts involved, the potential benefits to the business and themselves, and the new techniques and systems to be used;

- techniques practice, which should be carried out in small groups and where telephone enquiries are involved, actually over the phone with trainers and coaches;

- monitoring of prospects handling, carried out on a periodic and ongoing basis to ensure new methods are actually being put into practice;

- regular reviews of conversion rate results per individual, which are also vital.

The reason I have included this section in my 10 commandments is simple. It is because I have seen many organisations totally buy into all the concepts mentioned and then do absolutely nothing. They have attended my public seminars or invited me 'in-house' to speak or advise on this topic and then believed that hearing about it would somehow do the trick.

In the same way that reading about healthy eating and diet plans won't cause weight loss, merely reading up and hearing about my 'converting enquiries' material won't bring you new business. Start to ACT ... now!

10. Understand and master the five-step conversion process

While every business has slightly different requirements as regards personal interactions there are five common practical steps to dealing with every lead or enquiry. Get the relevant individuals implementing and mastering these, in the order I mention them, and you will see very quick and dramatic results.

Note that it is not my intention to give you word-for-word scripts. I don't like or believe in scripts. I want you to understand the underlying concepts and get your team to think its way through being able to create its own material around phrases and actions that team members feel personally comfortable with.

The five-step conversion process

Before I explain the simple five-step process, I want you to understand that there is a common theme and linguistic tool that runs through each step: that is the need for the powerful use of questions in any interaction with prospects. I actually refer to this as the 'ASK concept' of converting enquiries, as asking conversational questions is the basis to this technique.

There are three important reasons why the use of questions works far better than simply 'telling' the prospects things, or just blandly giving them information:

1 Whoever asks the questions controls the conversation.

2 Asking conversational questions controls the focus of what people think and feel.

3 A question commands a response. Think about it: if someone asks you a question, don't you instinctively feel compelled to give an answer?

Thus, regardless of whether you are dealing with an incoming telephone call, making an outgoing call to follow up a lead or having a personal meeting or visit from a prospect, your aim is the same. Through the skilful use of questions you are seeking to control the conversation, influence the prospect's focus and drive them towards the response that you desire.

Will this appear contrived and manipulative? No, because it is all done casually, helpfully with gentle, soft, conversationally natural questions. In fact, learn to do it well and you or your team won't even realise that you are doing it at all.

I also want you to take into account that this simple five-step system for converting enquiries is built around what I call the value v. price scales (see Chapter 3). This reflects my basic rule, which is to communicate as many value benefits as possible, before discussing the price.

As I explain each of the five steps, I will of course be giving general examples, but I can't possibly deal with every situation or business sector in the book. It will be up to you to work out how to apply the conceptual principles behind the various stages in your own business. If you have a problem with this, contact me and ask for help at ian@iancooper.co.uk

With these various points in mind, you are ready to put them into practice with the five-step conversion process.

Step one: invite your prospect into a conversation and set an agenda

Whether your prospect comes to you, via the telephone or face-to-face, your first step and objective is to engage them in a conversation. Most prospects will either make contact with a specific standard question, or in a retail environment they may simply just turn up and browse. You will hear questions like:

- 'How much?'
- 'Do you have ...?'
- 'Is it possible to ...?' etc. etc.

So how do you move them from their factual question to a conversation? Easy, you ask a question back. Remember, a question controls the conversation and focus and also triggers a response. If you simply give a price, or a flat, straight and direct answer to a question, you limit your chances of actually having a chat with them. That doesn't mean you need to be evasive, but what you need to do is to try to get the prospect to be prepared to share their needs, wants and if necessary personal issues with you if they are relevant to the purchase. You need to try to take control and invite them into a conversation.

So, for example, what happens if the prospect calls your piano tuning business and asks the most predictable of all questions ... 'How much?' You could simply give the answer ... '£50', but the call may then end with the prospect ringing around. If nothing else is raised, the likelihood is the prospect will choose the cheapest. However, instead of launching into standard price and fee information, flip things round and respond by asking them a question and effectively pull them into a conversation with their permission.

You could respond with something like this in a friendly and interested tone:

Prospect: I wonder if you can give me some indication of the cost of tuning a piano?

Handler: Absolutely … no problem … more than happy to help! But listen, are you okay for a few minutes so that I can get a little bit of background about what sort of piano you have, where you are based, your timescale and anything else I should know? Then I can give you the most appropriate figure and we can chat about when would be most helpful to get the job done. Is that okay?

Prospect: Yes, that is fine!

Now obviously this is just a random example, which might not be directly relevant to your situation (unless you happen to be a piano tuner), but it contains many elements that you can adapt almost universally. Let's see what has happened here:

- First of all, you will almost certainly have differentiated yourself from the majority of the competition. This immediately creates a good impression, reflecting your interest in them.
- By answering a question with a question, you have taken back control.
- By focusing their mind on what you are going to do and cover, you are effectively setting out an agenda.
- By asking 'Is that okay?' at the end and getting a positive response, you are getting their permission to proceed to have a conversation with them, where you will gather the information you require.

Step two: build rapport with the prospect

Building rapport is one of the hardest things to write about and describe. In this context, it means creating and making a personal 'connection' with the prospect. It is that intangible, almost unconscious, positive feeling that you want them to have, which will influence them in your direction. Let me offer a few tips on rapport building to play around with. Once you have invited yourself into a conversation and the prospect is happy to respond, you could consider asking in your most informal and chatty manner:

- questions that will enable you to respond with empathy and interest when you get their answers;
- questions that will elicit their personal state and emotions;
- questions that will get them to give you personal information, which you can then react to appropriately;

■ questions about what has triggered them being interested in your goods or services at this moment in their life;

■ questions that will probably trigger a bit more conversation.

So, for example, you may be:

■ a solicitor who finds out a prospect wants a will because they are going travelling for three months;

■ an optician who finds out a prospect wants contact lenses because they have just got a part in a play with an amateur drama group;

■ a seller of lawn mowers who finds out that the prospect has just moved house to somewhere with a bigger garden;

■ a seller of office furniture who discovers his prospect has just moved into larger office premises to expand.

In each of these cases, when the prospect has parted with this sort of information, you would be able to comment appropriately, chat about their circumstances and ask more rapport building questions ... *'Where are you travelling to?'* ... *'Wow, what play are you in?'* ... *'How big is the garden?'* ... *'Great to hear you are expanding, what business are you in?'*

This doesn't have to take long, but once you start getting these sorts of answers you are on your way to making that 'personal connection'. The closer you get to that, the more the prospect will want to go with you or your business and the harder it will be for them to go with someone else, even if you are a little more expensive. On an unconscious level, the connection you have begins to be a differentiating factor and a powerful 'weight block' in your favour, which may help minimise the importance of price.

I know what you are thinking. What happens if the prospect just wants direct answers and no chat? Fine, give them what they want and move forward to the next step in the five-step process. All you can do is try. Remember, you are not going to succeed every single time. All you are seeking to do is to do better than you (and probably most of your competitors) are currently doing in terms of conversion rates.

Step three: bounce back

Bouncing back is really easy to understand and to do. It is simply the process and technique of quite literally repeating back to the prospect, using their words as closely as possible, your understanding of what they want with any circumstances and details they have provided. This will have a positive influence by showing you have listened, understood their situation and mentally interpreted it in the same way as them. For example:

> 'So, Mrs Johnson, let me see if I have understood this correctly. What you are saying is that you are looking for a "book and sunbed" holiday for two adults in Paphos, at a four or five star hotel, going from East Midlands airport for 10 nights during September at a budget of up to £750 per person. Is that correct?'

Note, the expression *'book and sunbed'* holiday uses the prospect's phrase and the final question commands a response, which leads to the next step.

Step four: give the information requested

This is now the stage to explain and give the prospect whatever information they have requested, which of course may well include the price. Do it clearly, without hesitation and with as little technical or sector specific jargon as possible. Make sure you also ask feedback questions as you go along such as:

- 'Does that make sense to you?'
- 'Would that be helpful?'
- 'Have I explained that okay, or is there any part of it you want me to run through again?'
- 'Do you have any questions for me?'

Explore ways to deliver your information and price, with as many benefits as possible and to include as many elements as you can find, to add to the perceived value.

If you couple the rapport brought about through the first three steps of the process, with the value and benefits explained to the prospect, the more willing they will be to actively 'want' to go ahead with you at the price you want them to pay.

Step five: ask for what you want

One of the main reasons organisations don't get better conversion rates is simply because they don't ask for what they want. All too often I have heard experienced enquiry handlers 'iffing' the prospect away. It is very common to hear the phrase *'If you would like to go ahead, please don't hesitate to get back to us.'*

The moment the 'if' word is used, the enquiry handler is planting a message in the prospect's brain that this is not the time to make their mind up and to proceed to the next and final stage, whatever that may be.

If you want to get a higher conversion rate, then having followed the earlier steps, you must ask directly for the prospect's business or an appointment or whatever it is you are looking for. Note that at any future appointment or encounter you can and should use exactly the same five-step system and structure for that call or meeting to get your ultimate conversion to a sale.

Additional tips on this topic of sales and examples of how to overcome any objections that might arise are given in Chapter 8.

General tips on handling leads and enquiries

Handling e-mail enquiries

Many businesses now receive an increasing and significant number of e-mail leads and enquiries directly or via the web asking for prices or other information. Here is how to handle them:

1 If possible and practical, don't ignore them or simply respond to the e-mail with the costs figure or a standard information attachment.

2 If possible, you should do everything you can to ensure that the prospect has put their contact details on their enquiry, so you can try to speak to them and then use the five-step conversion process.

3 If this is not possible, or the volume is too great, then ensure that the written information that you do send to them is personal, influential and peppered with benefits and value 'weight blocks'. Even when writing to people, you can still seek to build rapport. (See Chapter 3 on pricing and Chapter 8 on writing skills.)

Avoid the use of jargon

Have you ever had your car serviced to be told by the mechanic that the 'triple threadle sprocket' needs replacing? Jargon is very intimidating. Whatever business sector you are in, there will be certain terms or an internal language that is used. Remember, if your prospects are from outside of your sector, speak to them in plain English.

Follow up a telephone enquiry in writing

Where a telephone enquiry has ended with the prospect indicating they will give it some thought, then if possible, tell them you will send them an immediate e-mail or letter confirming all that has been said.

Make it personal to the conversation, confirm what has been said, tell the prospect you would like to do business with them, put forward as many benefits as possible, repeat your price or fee information and then make it as easy as possible for them to say 'yes' to you.

I have seen businesses increase conversion rates by 10 per cent just by doing this! Why? It potentially differentiates you from your competitors, shows you are interested in the prospect and above all demonstrates you can keep your promises. You told them you would write to them and you have.

6

Priority 2 – Develop more business from existing customers and clients

Your existing customer and client base is money in the bank. Invest in it well and make it work for you.

With this in mind, the overall simple objectives of Priority 2 are to get existing customers and clients:

- to repeat their purchases and buy more of the same from you again;
- to buy additional goods and services from you;
- to spread positive word-of-mouth so others buy from you too.

This chapter explains my five golden rules for achieving these objectives and winning more profitable business from the customers and clients you already have.

THE FIVE GOLDEN RULES

1 Know your customers and clients.
2 Keep your customers and clients happy.
3 Keep in touch with customers and clients.
4 Offer additional products and services.
5 Get customers and clients to recommend and refer.

Golden rule 1 – Know your customers and clients

Too many people in business obviously believe they have super human powers and are able to remember every customer or client over the past 20 years. The truth is, of course, many can't remember a customer who returns after a week, let alone those who don't come back at all. Perhaps even more important and damaging is their perception that past customers and clients will remember them.

This isn't good enough. There is no excuse for not knowing who your customers are. To do this you either need to have an effective electronic CRM (customer relationship management) system or at the very least a simple manual system that works for you. This doesn't have to be expensive, but it must enable you to quickly access key information about your customers. This is not optional if you want to survive and prosper. Too many businesses are even failing to do the two most basic things:

1 Capture the names, addresses and contact details of their customers and clients.

2 Store them somewhere where they can be easily accessed and used for future business development.

For example, when was the last time a restaurant you have eaten in made any attempt to take your address or e-mail so that it could contact you again with offers and promotions? I have only ever been in two; both were small, independent businesses. They got my details without it feeling inappropriate. One simply had a card on the table to fill in to join its restaurant 'membership scheme', which offered a 10 per cent discount off future meals and various other offers. I enjoyed the meal and service, so why wouldn't I be interested in such an opportunity?

The other had a weekly competition to guess the name of a large soft toy on display in the restaurant entrance area. Winners would get the toy. Of course the entry cards, which had to be handed in, asked for names and e-mail details. Not only did the restaurant harvest many customers' details, but guessing the name of the panda became a sociable bit of fun to chat about over the meal.

Be creative and find a way to get the details of your customers. If you can't think of a clever scheme, simply be open and ask politely: *'Would you mind if I make a note of your contact details, so we can make you aware of future discounts, offers and new products?'* Some will say yes and others will decline, but I guarantee that just by asking you will get massively more than you would if you carry on doing nothing. I will come on to what you do with this information later on in this chapter in golden rule 3.

So what customer or client information should you try to get that might be useful in the future? It will of course vary according to the business, range of products or services and the sector, but in a perfect world the list below is a helpful start:

- names, address, phone and e-mail details;
- date of purchase of goods or services;
- what goods or services they bought;
- how much they spent;
- what activity brought them to you;
- last contact;
- next contact planned.

Of course, I recognise that in many cases the likelihood is that you will only be able to get a few of these things. The aim however is to be aware of the importance of this issue and do as much as you can, not as little.

My commissioning editor gave me a great example of how customer or client information should be used. She explained, 'Every year we go to the Knoll House Hotel in Purbeck, and every year they remember what newspaper we read, the name of our dog and son and the room we prefer. They do all this without it sounding like we're part of a database by saying things like: "Will Samba be coming with you this time?" That attention to detail runs through every aspect of the hotel, which is why I've been going there since I was a baby.'

Whatever information you have, your customer and client database or customer relationship management system should be regarded as the engine room of your future business development efforts.

Golden rule 2 – Keep your customers and clients happy

If you want an existing customer or client to do more business with you and recommend you to others, then they need to have been happy with you the first time around. While this seems extremely simple, many businesses take this notion for granted and the concept becomes something of a cliché not requiring any serious and planned action.

There is more to this, however, than simply selling quality goods or services. There are in fact three important things you must do over and above basic product quality control:

1   Understand the distinction between technical or product quality and service delivery quality.

2   Measure customer or client feedback.

3   Deal with complaints well when they do arise.

Technical/product quality v. service delivery quality

Too many businesses claim they keep their customers and clients happy because, as they put it: *'We supply quality products and services.'* A noble claim but even if it is true, this is far from the whole story. Customers and clients will, in most situations, take it for granted that any goods and services you sell them will be of a certain standard. How happy or satisfied they are, however, is more likely to be judged and influenced by their overall experience of dealing with you. In practice, this is often more about getting the little things right ... actually those things that all too often get missed or ignored.

Take the example of one major department store chain that commissioned a multi-million-pound facelift of several of its stores. It had a re-design with trendy colours and modern displays and promoted this new design and image with an expensive advertising campaign to generate business. Much local publicity surrounded each store as it launched its new look. Contrast this high-power approach with the facts. On the day of re-opening one of its stores with the spotlight well and truly on, I can report that customer toilets lacked locks, toilet paper, soap and towels. I was kept waiting at the 'pay desk' while two assistants, one of whom was chewing gum, continued their private conversation about their boyfriends and when I finally asked for advice about a particular product one assistant fled in panic and the other confessed her total ignorance about the products.

While I clearly can't lay down any hard and fast rules to be followed for every possible business, I have however created a generic customer and client service related checklist that you can use to stimulate discussion and to enable you to carry out some internal analysis.

Go through the checklist on the following pages to see how much work you really have to do. Obviously, not all questions will apply to all businesses. Simply grade the ones that do. Anything below a 'good' means you have some work to do and that customer or client service delivery satisfaction may be compromised.

I am also aware that these checklists are merely an internal tool. I will be saying more about getting feedback from customers and clients later in this section.

Customer and client visits to your premises/shop/office

Rate your business/firm/branch/department honestly by ticking the appropriate box.

How would you rate:	Good	Fair	Poor
Your opening hours for customers and clients?	❏	❏	❏
Any available directions/maps to your premises?	❏	❏	❏
The visibility and signage at your premises?	❏	❏	❏
The outside appearance of your premises?	❏	❏	❏
The inside appearance of your premises?	❏	❏	❏
The appropriateness of the dress of your staff?	❏	❏	❏
The appearance of any reception or entrance area?	❏	❏	❏
The availability of reading materials about the business?	❏	❏	❏
Availability of refreshments?	❏	❏	❏
Punctuality for appointments?	❏	❏	❏
The way you cater for child visitors?	❏	❏	❏
The way you cater for disabled visitors?	❏	❏	❏
The attitude and approach of your reception staff?	❏	❏	❏
Confidentiality and privacy?	❏	❏	❏
Appearance of any meeting rooms or areas?	❏	❏	❏
Your meet and greet policy?	❏	❏	❏
Your showing out policy?	❏	❏	❏
Your toilet and cloakroom facilities?	❏	❏	❏
Car parking?	❏	❏	❏

Telephone communications with customers and clients

Tick the appropriate box.

How would you rate:	Good	Fair	Poor
Opening hours for calls?	❏	❏	❏
Telephone answering facilities when closed?	❏	❏	❏
Effectiveness of getting caller through to the correct person?	❏	❏	❏
Friendliness of answering?	❏	❏	❏
Speed of telephone answering?	❏	❏	❏

	Good	Fair	Poor
Ability to listen to caller's requests?	❏	❏	❏
Switchboard/reception internal knowledge of the business?	❏	❏	❏
Message-taking skills of people answering the phone?	❏	❏	❏
Ability of call handler to deal with upset callers?	❏	❏	❏
Delivery of messages to correct person?	❏	❏	❏
Responding to messages?	❏	❏	❏
Offering call back when needed?	❏	❏	❏

Written communications with existing customers and clients

Tick the appropriate box.

How would you rate:	Good	Fair	Poor
Response time for replies to letters/e-mails?	❏	❏	❏
Presentation of your written communications?	❏	❏	❏
Quality and helpfulness of written customer client information?	❏	❏	❏
The extent to which careless written mistakes are minimised?	❏	❏	❏
Minimising the use of jargon?	❏	❏	❏
Customer and client friendly written style?	❏	❏	❏
Keeping your customers and clients up to date with ongoing issues?	❏	❏	❏

Your personal approach to customers and clients

Tick the appropriate box.

How do you think your clients would rate you on the following issues:	Good	Fair	Poor
As being thorough in your preparation to meet or see them?	❏	❏	❏
As being creative with solutions to problems?	❏	❏	❏
As showing real interest in them?	❏	❏	❏
As giving decisive advice?	❏	❏	❏
As being reliable at keeping promises?	❏	❏	❏
As listening properly to them?	❏	❏	❏
As conveying sympathy?	❏	❏	❏
In making them feel important?	❏	❏	❏
In going the extra mile for them?	❏	❏	❏
At being flexible to help them get what they need?	❏	❏	❏
Product knowledge about your various goods or services?	❏	❏	❏

Measure customer or client feedback

Let me repeat the basic principle ... if you want your existing base to do more business with you and recommend you to others, then customers need to have been happy the first time around. With this in mind, it is essential to go through the process of asking your customers what they think of you.

Over the years, I have asked many businesses, *'What do your customers and clients think of you?'* I get a frequent and common response, *'We like to think they are pretty satisfied.'* The operative phrase here of course is *'We like to think'*.

It isn't enough to *'just think'*. You must know for sure what customers and clients really do think of you and if there are any recurring negative themes that you can deal with.

The best way to get customer or client feedback is to provide them with some form of feedback mechanism, which you invite them to complete. Here are some basic tips for this:

- **Keep it short**. I've come across some businesses which have pages of questions for customers to complete. This is justified by their marketing or research people wanting feedback on every conceivable aspect of the business's product or service. The basic rule though is, the longer the questionnaire, the fewer responses you will get. My advice is to go for the minimum number of questions that will give you only the most important information.

- **Keep the mechanism simple**. Give your customers and clients the opportunity to respond simply by marking or ticking the appropriate answer, which might literally be a yes or no, or good, average, poor.

  The more you ask them, the less likely they are to respond at all. So for example asking them to write detailed explanatory notes on several questions is likely to be counter-productive. However, there is nothing wrong at the end with inviting them to give any further general comments or suggestions.

- **Make it quick and easy for them to return.** Assume for a second that you've been successful enough to get customers to fill in your questionnaire. If they now have to find an appropriate sized envelope, write your address on it, buy a stamp and remember to take it to the post, you will get only a limited number back. Find a way of minimising the number of steps involved. If there is a way for them to give you some immediate feedback online then use it – there are several survey companies online that will do this for you at a very reasonable cost.

▨ Consider **the questions you should ask.** As mentioned above, go out of your way to ask as few questions as possible. Here are the most important minimum ones to include:

▨ How would you rate the quality of the products or services you have bought?

▨ How would you rate the overall experience of dealing with us?

▨ Would you use us again?

▨ How many people have you spoken to about us in positive terms?

▨ How many people have you spoken to about us negatively?

▨ Can you think of anything we could do to improve?

(The above is not intended to be a model template for you to use as a feedback questionnaire. It is merely a list of some of the most important things to include. You should tailor the wording of your questions to be appropriate to your customer base and market sector.)

Deal with complaints well when they do arise

Here is a fact of being in business: you will get complaints. Simply accept the fact that from time to time things will go wrong and therefore you need a strategy to deal with such situations when the inevitable happens. Most companies think of any complaints handling process they have – some like to call it 'customer relations' – as a purely administrative function, one that drains resources and contributes little. If this is you, then it is time for a re-think.

Complaints can and should play an integral role in business development. Look at it this way, in most cases there are only two possibilities: either the customer or client has a genuine and perfectly valid complaint or problem, or they think they do. In either event, you have a problem that needs to be dealt with and that problem is not an administrative one. It is a massive business development issue!

Many businesses tell me, *'We're lucky, we don't get many complaints,'* and see this fact as a reflection of the success of their product or service offering. This notion is far from the truth. You probably don't know how many dissatisfied customers you have because whether you sell to individual consumers or to other businesses, a huge number of dissatisfied customers simply do not complain at all. Extensive and detailed research carried out by TARP (Technical Assistance Research Programs), the world's leading international research organisation specialising in customer service and complaints, reveals that:

■ only 1–5 per cent of consumers complain to management or headquarters;

■ 45 per cent of consumers complain to a front line representative and 75 per cent in business-to-business (B2B) transactions complain to someone on the front line;

■ 50 per cent of consumers encounter a problem but don't complain at all and 25 per cent in B2B don't complain at all.

The bottom line, therefore, is that you can assume that for every complaint you receive, there are many others you never hear about. Doubt this? How often have you been in a restaurant and been unhappy with something but not complained? Even if you have said something, how often have you ever formally written or spoken to senior management or in the case of a nationwide brand written to headquarters? You may have talked about doing so, but often simply not got around to it. So how easy is it do you think for senior managers to really know what is happening day-to-day in their business, especially about the things that are dissatisfying their customers?

Why is all this a business development issue? Three simple reasons. Dissatisfied customers or clients:

■ may stop buying from you altogether;

■ may stop recommending you to others;

■ will almost certainly spread negative word-of-mouth.

Additional research by TARP shows that a negative experience causes two to four times as much word-of-mouth as a positive experience. Given that for most organisations at least 25 per cent of new business is driven by word-of-mouth, any unknown and unresolved dissatisfaction can be expensive. Very expensive. Even more so in certain sectors where some businesses get as much as 75 per cent of their business from word-of-mouth.

One other fact to take into account. John Goodman of TARP, the 'guru' on this topic, has coined the expression 'word of mouse'. John has identified the fact that word-of-mouth on the web (word of mouse) is usually four times as great if it is negative, causing even greater damage.

So what happens if you can find out about problems and then resolve them to the customer's or client's satisfaction? More TARP research among thousands of businesses from a massive range of sectors over many years has revealed that:

■ soliciting and satisfying a complaint usually results in a 50 per cent increase in loyalty v. the unarticulated complaint;

■ moving a complainant from dissatisfied to completely satisfied raises loyalty by 30–50 per cent and produces significant positive word-of-mouth referrals – the source of 25–75 per cent of new customers;

■ customers who complain and are subsequently satisfied are up to 8 per cent more loyal than if they had never had a problem at all.

In practice, therefore, what all this means is that complaints handling *is* an important business development tool. With this in mind here are a few tips relating to complaints.

TIPS FOR DEALING WITH COMPLAINTS

■ Actively seek out and solicit complaints and feedback to identify which areas of your activity people are unhappy about. There is even research to support the fact that merely giving people a chance to get things off their chest increases business retention.

■ Reduce and minimise the number of complaints in the future by actively listening to your customer or client feedback.

■ Always assume initially that the customer is honest, right and acting in good faith.

■ Always listen and let dissatisfied customers have their 'say'.

■ Go the extra mile to deal with complaints, to show how seriously you take them. For example, get someone at the most senior level to call the complainant.

■ Apologise as often as you can. Even if you think the complainant is in the wrong, it is easy to say, *'I'm sorry you feel the way you do.'*

■ Always be respectful and never, ever be aggressive, minimise or ignore the importance of the complaint to the customer, even if it seems trivial. However minor it might appear, it is important to them. By way of example, I know of a professional services firm which aggressively dug its heels in over an individual complaint involving a small sum of money. Eventually, the unhappy client wrote to the papers. The report led to many others coming forward with a similar complaint about the same organisation. This led to the professional body getting involved with disciplinary investigations and procedures. The result ... some of the senior people in that organisation being suspended from practising. All because they mismanaged the complaint at the outset.

■ Align with dissatisfied customers. Show them you understand how they feel.

■ Ask unhappy customers and clients what they would like you to do about the problem.

> ■ If it is practical, do it and do it quickly. If you can't, be polite and offer as much as you can in recompense.
>
> ■ Only allow the problem to escalate after all else has failed.

Golden rule 3 – Keep in touch with your customers and clients

Isn't it a fact that as a customer or client there are many businesses you have dealt with that you have never heard from since your purchase? In many cases this will be because many businesses simply don't know who you are and haven't thought to ask for your contact details. However, there are just as many which will have your details but will still never contact you. They haven't made the connection that keeping in touch produces more new business, without the cost of external promotion or marketing.

For example, when was the last time an independent travel agent, decorator, carpet fitter, furniture supplier, taxi firm, solicitor, electrician, car repairer, electrical goods supplier, builder, etc. that you have bought goods or services from over the years has been in touch with you since you dealt with them? In most cases, despite the fact that they will inevitably have your details, they will rarely have been in touch with you.

Let me tell you what you should be doing. You should be striving to achieve what I call the concept of 'customer or client ownership'. Customer or client ownership is the holy grail of business development when it comes to your existing base and it should be treated extremely seriously.

You need to adjust your thinking and philosophy so that those you have done business with are regarded not only as past customers or clients but also future ones with whom you have a continuing relationship … essentially customers and clients that you, as a business, own.

Your aim is to create the perception in the mind of your customers and clients that you are their solicitor, travel agent, car repairer, decorator, hotel, etc. You are on the way to achieving this when they know that you regard them as your customer or client.

Putting your name in front of them on a regular basis, through some form of communication, goes a long way to fostering this perception. Otherwise many people simply have to start from scratch each time when choosing their suppliers because they can't remember who they used last time and therefore feel no loyalty or connection to them.

Let's put it to the test: which law firm did you use last time you moved home? What is the name of the person you dealt with? The chances are that unless you moved very recently, you won't remember. Had that firm or person been in touch with you a few times a year ever since, assuming you were happy with them, you would most likely regard them as your lawyers and think of them first in the event that a legal requirement cropped up.

> Antwiss Engineering is a small, independent, car servicing business. Every year like clockwork they drop a note to their customers to remind them when a service or MOT is due. Not only does this ensure that they are the first port of call for regular car maintenance, but they are seen as helpful to customers who are often too busy (or forgetful) to remember when their car needs a service.

Many businesses complain that past customers and clients go elsewhere. The truth is, however, that if your business, department, office or branch allows the months and years to go by without any contact at all, you only have yourself to blame when they can't remember you or are unaware of the other services that you might be able to offer them.

Here is a menu of possible activities for keeping in touch. Choose the ones that are most appropriate to your business and style of approach.

A MENU OF KEEPING IN TOUCH ACTIVITIES

▨ Ask them for satisfaction feedback about your goods or services.

▨ E-mail them news about your business. If you have moved premises, appointed new people, developed a new product range ... tell them. For example, I received an e-mail recently from a hotel I stayed in over a year ago, telling me how they have just put new luxury mattresses in every room in the hotel. Mario Fijalkowski, director of the Coronas Playa Hotel in Lanzarote, one of the Thomson Gold package hotels, articulated the 'keeping in touch' concept perfectly when he explained to me: *'We communicate with our guests several times each year, so that it makes it hard for them to forget us. It is this policy, together with our recruitment of staff with the right people skills, that is responsible for us getting as high as 87 per cent repeat returning guests at one point last year.'*

▨ E-mail them appropriate information that might be of interest and help. For example, if you sell cameras or process and print photographs, send customers articles or useful links about how to take great pictures. If you are an accountant, update your clients on any tax changes.

▨ Send regular newsletters and updates to keep up the communications momentum.

▨ Send time-appropriate reminders: for example, opticians and dentists should be reminding patients when it's time for a check-up. Gardeners should be reminding customers when it is time to be doing certain things in the garden. Vets should be reminding owners when their pets' vaccinations are due.

▨ Connect and communicate with useful content on social media. (See Chapter 7.)

■ Create and establish a special group on LinkedIn and invite customers and clients to join.

■ Create and join your existing customer base to some form of loyalty scheme. This is something businesses of all sizes can do. You will all be familiar with the big retailers like Tesco and their various loyalty points systems. However, there is no reason why small organisations can't use the same concept. Even my local high street retailer of printer ink cartridges has her own scheme offering free refills after so many cartridges purchased.

■ Depending on the nature of your business it might be appropriate to meet customers and clients socially in order to discuss existing and future business.

■ Organise seminars or events to which customers can be invited. Make sure that you open these to the contacts of those you invite as well.

■ Make 'how are things going?' calls. I have, in the past, depending on the sector, encouraged some of my clients to call their customers and clients and simply ask: 'How have things been going since that…?' Apart from the goodwill this creates, I can tell you that in approximately 50 per cent of these calls the customer responded with: 'Actually while you're on the phone there is something that we might need your help with…'

■ Make 'how are things going?' visits. This is essentially the same as above, but it involves you actually paying your customer or client a personal visit. Clearly you have to be selective about who you target for this contact, but in such situations I have found that in approximately 70 per cent of these visits the client will actually find another bit of business to offer you.

■ Write to specific segments of your base offering them special deals, discounts or packages.

■ Offer occasional big gestures. My wife and I were on a flight to the US a few years back for a 30th wedding anniversary trip. It was a special holiday that had been organised by a local and independent travel agent. Halfway through the flight we were presented with a bottle of champagne from this agent who had arranged this gesture specially. It was an unexpected goodwill gesture and contact. We hardly ever make a trip now without giving this agent a chance to book it.

In general, before indulging in expensive external business development activities, always start out by approaching the top 20 per cent of your existing base first and then following up with the remaining 80 per cent.

MORE TIPS ON KEEPING IN TOUCH

■ **Frequency of contact.** It needs to be often enough to make sure the customer or client makes the connection that they are yours, but without spamming them or overdoing the contact. Clearly some sectors offer up more possibilities than others. I don't want to hear from my dentist every week, but I might well be open to some useful information from a business guru on a weekly basis.

Clearly there are no hard and fast rules about this but as a rough guide if you were to aim for a minimum of four times a year you would be able to meet most of your objectives without too much resistance.

■ **Be selective.** Using your client or CRM system, database or list, be highly selective. Segment your base and be careful to tailor your contact methods to be as relevant, appropriate and helpful as possible to those you are contacting.

■ **Be personal.** By all means automate the process, but the more you can personalise it or create the illusion of it being personalised, the better.

■ **Be brief.** Most of your customers and clients will be busy like you, so get to the point in any communications. I have had examples where a three-line piece of information has massively outperformed three pages, even though the three pages have far more content.

■ **Be helpful.** Always make sure that anything you send to an existing customer or client is presented in such a way that it appears to be helpful to them and to carry a direct potential benefit.

■ **Focus on building relationships.** Don't make the subject of every communication a blatant and direct sales pitch. Build an ongoing relationship with the customer or client based on their needs by providing them with useful information.

■ **Ask them to buy and tell them how.** If the purpose of a specific communication is to get the customer or client to buy something from you then be specific about that and give them easy steps to be able to do so immediately.

Golden rule 4 – Offer additional products and services

Whatever product or service you sell your customers, there is almost always something else you can offer them. This is known as cross selling, or 'upselling', and is one of the most neglected business development tools and concepts.

Businesses talk about it a lot, but often do little in any structured or planned way. If you are one of the businesses doing it, then it is worth exploring what else you can do. If you are not yet focusing on this area, you should know that it offers you huge potential to get 'free' extra business and revenue. It is one of the easiest and cheapest ways to develop your business.

Think about it for a second. The hard part is already done, you already have the customer. It is far easier to get them to do more with you than to find another new one altogether.

Here then are a few practical tips to enable you to sell additional products and services to your existing base of customers and clients.

Don't label or define the customer or client by what they have bought in the past

I know a travel agent who talks about his 'cruise' passengers, or a firm of solicitors which refers to its 'wills' clients. Thinking of them in this way is not constructive. They are simply customers and clients who may buy a wide range of other goods and services from you if you approach them and ask them in the right way.

Communicate your full range of products and services to your existing customer and client base

Here is a worrying fact: many customers and clients of your business will sometimes buy certain goods or services from competitors that they could have bought from you. Ask them why. There is one answer that will pop up more than any other: 'Oh, I didn't know you did that.'

> For example, I know of a business with a great reputation for bespoke fitted bedrooms, which loses potential kitchen fitting work from happy customers because it hasn't told them it does that as well. Similarly, I know of an accountancy firm which has had a client for over 10 years for auditing services but hasn't told them of several of its add-on business and IT consulting services.

With this in mind you must take advantage of every opportunity you can to make your existing base fully aware of the full range of things on offer. For example:

- Display a list on your premises.
- Use any reception or waiting areas to present information.
- Display headings in windows and other public areas.
- Give your existing customers and clients appropriate pieces of promotional and informational material.
- List everything on your website.
- Print them on your business cards. (The back is normally blank so use the space.)
- Print general headings on your stationery, invoices and letter paper.
- Mention key headings on your e-mail signature and sign-offs.
- Ensure your own staff and team know your entire services and product range.

Be creative and identify what else you can offer your existing base

Sit down right now and make a list of additional items that you can offer your existing base. Don't hold back, get as many things on the list as possible regardless of whether they are obvious or outrageously unconventional. Be free and creative with your thinking. The following list includes some fairly obvious ones and a few outside the norm. I can't cover all businesses; the list is just meant to be illustrative and to stimulate your thinking. If you get stuck, e-mail me for more points that relate to your business or sector.

- electrical retailers selling extended warranties;
- travel companies selling holiday insurance;
- cycle shops selling helmets with bikes;
- shoe shops offering suede and leather cleaning products;
- toy shops selling batteries with toys;
- bookshops and garden centres selling teas and coffees;
- greengrocers providing celebration baskets of fruit by delivery;
- hotels selling beds and soft furnishings in the room;
- coffee machine companies selling coffee and brand-name mugs;
- electricians selling lightbulbs so customers have spares;
- foreign exchange dealers selling holiday items like suitcases and travel accessories;
- mobile phone retailers offering protective cases with phones;
- carpet sellers and fitters offering cleaning services in a year's time;
- dentists selling toothbrushes and mouthwash;
- vets selling pet food and accessories;
- pharmacists selling basic health testing services such as blood pressure tests;
- solicitors who do divorce work or conveyancing offering their clients will writing.

Often the easiest peg to hang your creative thinking on is: what is the purpose behind the customer or client's initial purchase? It is even more opportunistic to think about how you can use your customer visits or footfall, your own space or your own database to sell additional goods or services of different types to your existing customers:

■ **Visitors or footfall.** I recently came across a newsagent selling papers and the usual newsagency fare. Knowing he had volume visits and 'footfall' from existing customers, he was generating extra income out of his main base by taking and producing passport pictures in his shop. He would pull down a screen with a plain background, take pictures himself with a digital camera and print off a set of six passport pictures in the back. He even offered customers coffee while they waited.

■ **Space.** WH Smith now utilises its space and footfall in a large number of its stores offering legal services from national legal brand QualitySolicitors.

■ **Database and membership.** The AA now leverages plumbing and home services such as boiler repairs.

What can you think of?

Ask your existing base to buy

If you don't ask customers and clients to buy some add-on product or service, then they probably won't, and you will miss out on a large amount of easily winnable potential business. It isn't just enough to decide what items or services you may be able to cross sell and to intellectually understand the concept. You have to encourage all your people to be active and to ask directly.

Golden rule 5 – Get customers and clients to recommend and refer

How do you feel when you get a call from someone who says, 'You have been recommended by …'? You should feel great, for a couple of reasons. Firstly, it means someone has been so satisfied with the previous sale that they have enough faith to recommend you. Secondly, this business lead or opportunity is free. You simply have to convert it now into profitable business.

Now let me ask you another question. How do you feel when recommending people or businesses to others? It also makes you feel good, doesn't it? You actually derive a sense of satisfaction, pleasure and significance from helping others with your recommendations.

The anomaly, however, is that despite businesses wanting recommendations, referrals and introductions and people liking to give them, too many businesses sit back and simply wait for things to happen. Stop waiting! You can stimulate referrals and introductions within your business by adopting a few relatively simple strategies. Obviously some are more suited to specific sectors and business types, so mix and match from any of the following.

Say thank you

When you do get an introduction from someone, make sure you contact the person it comes from and say a sincere thank you. This isn't just an old-fashioned clichéd courtesy, it is good business development practice. The more you show your gratitude or appreciation, the more likely the other party will be to do it again.

Ask directly for introductions and referrals

When someone tells you how much they like your goods and services, ask them outright: *'Thank you so much. Do you know anyone else who might have a similar requirement that you can introduce us to or we can contact on your recommendation?'* If you've never done this, you'll be surprised how often it produces positive results.

Get into your contacts' 'contacts circle'

How many people do you know: 50, 100, 200, 1,000? It doesn't matter, the point is we all have our own personal and business contact circles. If you provide helpful and useful informational material to your contacts via e-mail, blogs or other social media networking platforms, the likelihood is that it will be spread throughout their contact circles too. They effectively become your indirect sales force.

Create business introduction incentive schemes

Providing you are ethically and legally allowed, consider introducing some form of incentive scheme to get your existing customers, clients, contacts or even staff to introduce you to new leads. This really works well. I recently had two social contacts of mine arguing over which of them was going to introduce me to a particular company in order to get their £50 gift voucher, if and when I signed up. Note it doesn't even have to be a monetary incentive. I've come across schemes where people are rewarded internally through other prizes or even internal awards.

Seminars and events

If you are inviting your existing customers and clients to any events or seminars you're putting on, allow them to bring guests. This has many benefits. It means invited individuals are more likely to come if they have company, invited businesses can be made to look good if they are able to bring customers or clients of theirs to your event, and of course it directly introduces you to new prospects who immediately become grateful to you.

Have a formal referral analysis programme

In many sectors it is the commercial norm to seek to foster the mutual referral of business. For example, there is a high level of reciprocity between solicitors, accountants and banks. The same applies between car dealers and body shop repairers. If you are in a business sector that gives and receives referrals, then start monitoring who you are giving work to, so you can review these gifts of business against who you are getting business from.

Play referral swapping games with your competitors over non-competing services

There will be occasions when you may offer some products or services that some of your competitors don't have and vice versa. Explore ways of exchanging these.

Get involved in formal referral activities

There are many local and regional referral networks and clubs, and others that are run by various social and business groups. Depending on the kind of business you are in and your own personal skills, aim to participate in these as they can be well worth joining.

Get active in social media networking sites

This activity is hugely important, so much so I have written a whole section on it. (See Chapter 7.)

A final question on Priority 2

If your competitors think it is worth investing in targeting your customer and client base ... why don't you?

7

Priority 3 – Externalise business development efforts to generate new opportunities, leads and enquiries

If you have just skipped here without reading Chapters 5 and 6 I'm going to emphasise again that there is little point in investing in external activities until you have mastered the art of converting as many of your existing leads into profitable business as possible and until you put in place strategies to get more business from your existing base. Getting your priorities right is crucial.

Once you've done that it's time to look at filling up the 'enquiries or leads bucket', mentioned earlier. There are many business development activities that will drive potential customers or clients to you. I will focus here on those that I believe to be the most practical and important in terms of cost.

Yes, I could tell you to set aside some cash for TV advertising or sponsoring a Premier League football team, but my gut feeling is that most of my readers haven't got a spare million or two to play with. With this in mind, here are my top five external activities for winning profitable customers and clients. The sections in this chapter discuss each in detail:

- the internet: the commonsense guide to developing your business online;
- 14 ways to develop your business through joint ventures and collaboration;
- how to win in competitive situations;

- brand your way to business success;
- how to win business by direct telephone targeting.

The internet: the commonsense guide to developing your business online

When it comes to the online business development world, I regularly encounter four types of people and businesses: business 'techno junkies', 'techno masters', 'techno dabblers' and 'techno dinosaurs'.

The 'techno junkies' love the online world a bit too much. They positively drool over the technical process and doing things online is almost more important to them than the results they get. They believe that unless it is happening online using the most modern spec, it is not happening at all!

The 'techno masters' are holders of business development internet 'black belts'. Whether they enjoy it or not, they appreciate the potential and they have developed the 'know how' and commercial 'nouse' to leverage and exploit the online world to their financial and business advantage.

The 'techno dabblers' understand the importance of online business development, but jump in and out with the odd unplanned bit of activity here and there and often kid themselves that they know what they are doing.

Finally we have the business 'techno dinosaurs', who proudly try to ignore the online world all together, because it is just 'too modern', 'not serious', 'not appropriate', 'too high tech', 'too time consuming to learn' and just plain 'not real business at all'! Speaking to such a specimen recently, I was told: *'The best thing about my computer screen is that I have something to stick my Post-it notes to!'*

Being a 'techno dinosaur' is not the smart option. In fact, it is not really an option at all. If this is you, then you are almost certainly missing out and losing potential business to your competitors and risk, like your namesake, becoming extinct.

We are experiencing a business revolution that is much more than a passing phase and we are witnessing a transformation in the business development world. The internet and the exponential growth of social media platforms means that every business has the potential to reach its target market on a global scale, 24 hours a day with almost pinpoint accuracy and in many cases for free, quite literally at the click of a button.

If you know how to leverage the power of this modern technology, the corner shop, the 'one-man' band and the creative entrepreneur working from her back bedroom can build very successful businesses to compete against the international mega brands with their huge resources.

The world is already full of 'gurus' writing very useful 'how to' manuals about YouTube, Twitter, Facebook, LinkedIn, etc. and similarly there are literally several thousand self-appointed internet marketing experts producing excellent articles, materials and courses on generating business online. This book does not set out to compete with these.

In order to be as helpful as possible in the context of a general book, I want to actually take a step back from the almost manic hype that surrounds this area and give the techno 'junkies', 'dabblers' and 'dinosaurs' some basic, pragmatic and commonsense tips that all too often get missed.

To start with, let's park for a while the technology and mechanics behind the online business world and take a look at some of the really basic questions I often get asked by the business community:

■ What are the potential benefits and opportunities of the online business development world?

■ What is holding me back from serious online business development activities?

■ How can I use social media networks to win profitable customers and clients?

■ What makes a good or bad website?

■ How do we generate website traffic?

■ What are the most common traps in using the online world?

What are the potential benefits and opportunities of the online business development world?

Visibility and prospects finding you

Let's suppose you have a business meeting in Hull with a business prospect and you want to eat in a halfway decent vegetarian restaurant in the city centre. How would you locate such a place?

I'm going to take a wild guess that if there was nobody you knew who could immediately give you the information, you would do one of two things:

1 You would hit the computer with a search, most likely on Google.

2 If you knew how, you would use social media networks to ask around.

Traditionally most external business development has revolved around you as a business actively looking for and trying to track down potential customers and clients. However, using your website and various social media networking platforms, the role is potentially reversed. The online world now makes it easy for those who are in the market for what you sell to come looking for you. All you have to do is simply help them find you and then turn any leads into business.

The bottom line is this: if your instinct is to use these methods to find what you are looking for, then others seeking the kind of goods or services you provide will be doing the same. If you are not there to be found, don't be shocked if you get missed and prospects go to competitors who have a proper presence online and who are doing more than 'dabbling' to get noticed.

Comparatively cheap or free

Whereas most traditional external business development activities can be very expensive with a high degree of wastage, much of what you can do online is comparatively cheap and with most social media networks actually free.

This means of course that you can sustain consistent efforts over long periods of time that would be almost impossible if you relied on funding traditional media advertising in newspapers, magazines, on radio or on TV.

Credibility and relationship building

Using the internet and social networking sites you are able to build up and develop credibility and relationships with prospects, professionals, like-minded people and potential introducers to a level that would be impossible any other way.

Control and analysis

'I know half of my advertising works ... I just don't know which half.'

This is a very famous quote in the advertising world, although curiously enough it is actually credited to various people. Whoever said it and however true it was in the past, or still is as regards traditional business development activities, in the online business development world it is no longer as relevant. With various analytical tools you can very precisely track and analyse which activities are working online and which aren't. You can then cut out the ineffective activities immediately.

The online world offers you a unique opportunity to experiment and play and only do that which gives you great results.

Precision targeting

> I read a full-page, colour advert yesterday in one of the weekend quality newspapers for a fantastic looking chainsaw. Wow, the copy and advert were so good that even I, who can't cut straight with a pair of scissors, was by the end of the advert positively lusting for this high-powered chain saw, despite the fact that I don't need one and will never buy one!

I mention this only because I was struck by the contrast between the great copy and what I know will be a very high degree of advertising wastage in terms of both targeting and cost.

Perhaps one of the most fantastic things about developing your business online and particularly via social media networks is the ability to target with a reasonable degree of precision. Gone are the days when you just pay through the nose to get your message out there. Now you can communicate with those you know are most likely to be interested in your various offerings. More on this later.

Passive income through a global presence 24 hours a day

Your online presence is accessible globally 24 hours a day. This means that the usual physical barriers created by geography and time zones are now meaningless and that you are potentially open for business while you are asleep.

> For example, I woke up one morning and found that I had done business in the US relating to an e-book I had written. Folk in the US had read information about it on a LinkedIn group I had contributed to, visited the relevant website link, paid for it online via PayPal and had it delivered, instantly, by download. I also now have the details of the purchasers so that I can, with their permission, make them aware of other relevant services and products. That is the power of the online business development world.

What is holding me back from serious online business development activities?

As you can see, the benefits of using the online world to develop your business are absolutely compelling, yet some business people are still not convinced. Let's explore the most common reasons I hear.

'It is just too techie for me . . . I just don't understand technology'

If you fall into this category, it's a bit like saying, 'I won't drive because I don't understand the mechanics of a car.' Despite your lack of mechanical know how you were shown which pedals to press and how to change gear. Likewise with internet business development and use of social media there will always be somebody out there to teach you what to do and how to do it. If that doesn't work there are many people out there who will simply do it for you. Whatever the cost, it will be far less than the amount of business you will potentially lose by doing nothing.

It is too time consuming

Saying it is too time consuming is like a medieval commander, about to lead his archers into battle, turning down the possibility of automatic machine guns on the grounds he is too busy to learn how to use them.

Providing you develop your understanding of the online world, learn how it can be used for the benefit of your business, have a proper plan and strategy, which spread the load and automate whatever is sensible, you should not rule out the online world on time grounds.

It is not relevant to my business

Whatever your sector or operation, don't ignore the potential of the online world to grow your business. Regardless of whether you're selling services or goods, you have the opportunity to broaden your target market by selling online.

Suppose, for example, you have a small specialist engraving business operating out of a small shop on the high street in Scunthorpe. You are physically limited by the local community's requirements for plaques, trophies, signs and corporate items. However, online you can display if you wish your entire product range, take engraving orders, payment in advance and then have your products shipped to customers' addresses that you will have a permanent record of.

Apart from the cost and maintenance of the website and time spent either keeping it up to date yourself or outsourcing this, you have potentially created a nationwide or even international business from your small premises.

If you can appreciate the potential, but are still deterred by any concerns over how you would market your business online, it is worth considering selling your products or services via eBay, which effectively does your marketing for you.

eBay already has over 100 of the major brand names selling goods and services via its website and over 180,000 small and medium-sized businesses are boosting their revenues through this source, with a good proportion of new business coming internationally. Ask yourself the big question: how can I use the online world to develop my business?

I'm too old . . . this stuff is for the youngsters

Focus on your business and not on you. It doesn't matter whether you like it or not, the real question is, are your potential customers and clients using the online world? If so, then you need to be there. Even Saga, that exists for the over 50s, very successfully offers a range of services and products online and has a very significant presence on social media networks.

We are worried what our people may say online that is damaging

Worrying about what your team might say on various social media networks is a genuine concern, but it should not be allowed to get in the way. After all, you trust your personnel to speak to members of the public over the phone or at your premises. Social networking is just another method of communication.

The answer to this concern is to have a plan and policy in place, which clearly set down some rules and internal standards over what can or can't be done online. If you've recruited the right people and trained them well they will be able to do this brilliantly for you.

Liberty of London experimented with Twitter by employing a bright young university student over the Christmas holidays. It chose the person with care, someone who represented the values of the business and had a passion for its products. He started to monitor Twitter, Facebook and various blogs relating to the products Liberty sold. He noticed an influential fashionista complaining that she couldn't get hold of a pair of tights that were the 'must-have' item of the moment. He went to the stockroom, found the tights and tweeted her to say he had them on hold for her. She collected them that day, wore them to a glamorous fashion event that evening and the next day wrote a post on her very popular blog about how amazing Liberty is and what great customer service it offers.

How can I use social media networks to win profitable customers and clients?

I have recently shared a number of speaking engagements with Heather Townsend, author of *The Financial Times Guide to Business Networking*, where Heather deals with this topic with great clarity and practical common sense. With kind permission from Heather, in order to answer this question, I am going to share with you her concept of the '4 Cs' with some explanation, examples and tips of my own. The '4 Cs' are:

- content
- connections
- conversation
- call to action.

Follow this step-by-step process and the strategic thinking behind it and it will lead you to another 'C' … customers and clients.

Content

Don't just dive straight in by randomly putting things on Facebook, Twitter, LinkedIn and YouTube or other platforms. Instead, stand back and take some time to develop a solid bank of content. This should be material and ideas with really useful, helpful information about your sector, services, products and expertise that can be posted over a sustained period of time. Do not make them overtly promotional. Whatever you sell, just focus on what your targets will find of genuine value and interest.

So, to extend the rather specialist and somewhat bizarre chainsaw example mentioned earlier, the company concerned could have a 'contents bank' of useful informational material to post that might include:

- tips on how to choose a chainsaw;
- how to start them;
- how to store them;
- how to clean them;
- how to use them effectively;
- technological advances in chainsaws;
- tips on relevant safety issues;
- what accessories are essential, e.g. gloves, goggles.

By posting this type of content, you are positioning yourselves as credible experts who people come to first and who can be trusted to know about chainsaws.

Connections

Once you've identified your content, you need to decide where your targets actually hang out. To continue the chainsaw example, search on LinkedIn for groups and communities relating to tree cutting, farming, gardening, landscaping, woodland issues etc. I have checked and there are many, many of them. If you run a general search on the web you will also find numerous forums on gardening and landscaping. Take a look on Twitter and you will also find lots of 'tweets' about related subjects.

Before doing anything else spend a bit of time reading the various discussions and forums before contributing with any of your content. Once you have found the most relevant then connect with some of these groups so that you become part of these communities. By the way, you don't have to join and contribute to all of them at once. Try a few to begin with and learn the ropes.

Conversation

Now you have some content at your disposal and you have found your communities, it is time to use your content to join in the conversation with your own contributions.

A WORD OF WARNING

Do not simply regard your contribution as a blatant sales or advertising platform. Remember, this is a conversation. You wouldn't just walk up to someone in a room and read them your advertising copy. You would seek to build up some rapport and trust first before moving things gently towards business if you felt there was some real interest.

What you are seeking to do on social media networks is to gradually create awareness of your brand and credentials and of your willingness to be helpful in a particular business sector. If you are patient and do these things well then it will influence others to trust you and to want you or your products and services.

I recommend you think in terms of what I call the 'conversational contribution quadrant'™. I believe there are four types of conversational contributions to be made to social media networks and you should roughly split them to reflect 25 per cent input, efforts and attention to each of these areas.

Figure 7.1 The conversational contribution quadrant

Ask questions	Give valuable information
Answer questions	Provide personal/product information

1 **Ask questions.** Using your content bank of topical burning issues in your sector, ask questions or raise topics which you know will provoke reaction and discussion from within your relevant communities.

2 **Give valuable information.** In order to build relationships and your credentials, give away information and tips before you look for direct gain yourself. With this in mind, post links to valuable and substantive information that your community will find helpful. This is again where you can use your content bank prepared earlier.

These links could be to blogs you have set up, which is a great way of fostering interaction and trust, or articles, useful websites and clips on YouTube that might be yours or belong to other people or businesses.

3 **Answer questions.** Remember, all effective conversations involve a two-way process. Where you see questions and comments posted by others for discussion that you could respond to, do so quickly and frequently.

4 **Provide personal/product information.** Providing your contributions are congruent with previous postings, it is fine and indeed desirable that you also have contributions about your business, product developments and special deals that are on offer to community members. Resist the temptation to do too much of this too soon. Remember, no more than 25 per cent of your postings should fall into this category and not until after you have contributed with the other elements of the quadrant first.

Call to action

In each of your postings, regardless of which section of the contribution quadrant you're dealing with, always have a call to action. In other words, invite the reader or recipient to do something. This might be to respond with additional content, to visit your website, to link or download something or of course even to buy, if it is appropriate.

What makes a good or bad website?

Use the CPS™ Approach. All too often I find it astonishing that many businesses ignore basic rules and tools of influence and good promotional communications in their quest for technical website wizardry and functionality. The CPS acronym is a simple guide to help keep you on track when it comes to putting your website together. It is a way of remembering what is most important.

C = customer or client

This is a reminder to make sure that first and foremost the customer is your priority and at the centre of everything you say and do on your website. The most important thing to keep in mind is what your prospective customers' needs, wants and emotional concerns are. Too many websites focus just on their services and products. Of course these should be present, but it should not be the basis of the entire site.

> For example, let's suppose you are in the laser eye surgery business. Simply showing a picture of your premises, with a bullet point list of your various procedures, falls short of what you should be doing. Ask yourself the following questions:
> ■ Why might somebody be considering this process?
> ■ What is their emotional state when they are thinking about the procedure?
> ■ What emotional state will they want to be in when it's been completed?
>
> These are the issues that should drive the crafting and language of the website, along with of course the details of what you offer.

P = people

Remember, 'people buy people first'. With this in mind if specific individuals or people are involved in your business, then the more appropriate and relevant information you are able to give about them, their skills, results and style and approach, the better. Essentially the more of a human face you're able to present, the greater the level of influence your website will have. Even if you are running a small family restaurant, or have a small retail fashion shop, the more you're able to present the individual people behind the business, the stronger the potential emotional connection will be.

With this in mind set up blogs, show photographs and biographical details and even better show short video clips on your website.

S = specialisation

Always remember, people buy in order either to solve their problems or to meet their specific needs and wants. With this in mind the more your website can appear to specialise in their concerns and desires, the better it will be. It will also make it easier for others to find you on search engines. Ask yourself when constructing your web presence how you can position yourselves as specialists.

For example, suppose you have a shop selling ladies' dresses for party and formal wear. Here are a few things you could do to create the feel of real specialisation:

■ Find and register specialist website domains for certain types of products, for example www.motherofbridedresses.com or www.special partyfrocks.com.

■ Have special landing pages for any such domains.

■ Create and promote a blog about these areas.

■ Create articles and put useful information on your site perhaps about current fashions, style, colours that work best with certain complexions, different manufacturers, etc.

■ Show video clips highlighting how dresses can be fitted and altered to fit.

Always remember why people visit websites. People visit websites for one of three reasons: either to buy something then and there, get information or advice on a topic, or for entertainment of some type. You need to make sure that your site does one or more of these three things.

Don't distract visitors with pointless technical design features. I come across far too many websites that have been designed by 'techno junkies'. These are people who go out of their way to use every conceivable 'gizmo' and function at their disposal for no other reason than they can. There is nothing more distracting than trying to read potentially influential copy while pop-ups, moving animated figures, sound effects and changing graphics keep getting in the way. Just keep it simple.

Include certain things on every page. One of your objectives should be to make navigating your site as easy as possible and therefore there are four things that should appear on every page:

1 contact information (e-mail, telephone or both);

2 menu information;

3 a direct link back to your home page;

4 a reminder of your call to action.

Make the site easy to read. Here are a few very simple tips:

- Have plenty of clear space on your pages.

- Don't clutter your page with too much information or dense text.

- Don't have a dark coloured text on a dark background or very light coloured text on a very light background.

Don't forget it is all about converting enquiries. Getting zillions of visitors to your site is often seen as the holy grail of internet business development, but getting them there is rather pointless if you don't then get them to do what you want.

You should recall the three priorities mentioned earlier in the book and that Priority 1 is the need to focus on converting enquiries into profitable business. This holds good for the online world too. You must give this as much, if not more, thought and importance as website design and copy content. To aid the conversion process here are a few tips:

- Harvest a database of prospects to whom you have given useful content and information, in return for them filling in a simple form with their contact details.

- Build a relationship with them through keeping in touch with them on a regular basis with more information that will help.

- Build personal credibility by showing video clips of your people talking about your goods and services.

- Build word-of-mouth through social media networks, to get those you are in touch with to spread the word about your business.

- Get them interacting with you through a blog.

- Build functionality, which makes it easy to buy from you.

- Give contact details frequently.

- Have calls to action mentioned frequently.

How do we generate website traffic?

There are three general methods and issues to be addressed and considered. You must decide which is most appropriate to your style, operation and comfort zone.

1 General search engine optimisation (SEO)

There isn't a day that goes by without somebody, somewhere, wanting to tell me how they can boost my natural rankings on the internet. By that I mean those that I am not paying for directly. Of course there are many genuine businesses out there with some real IT geniuses who do know their way around various internet search engines and who can guide you, at a price.

From a business development perspective I have an aversion to this paid-for solution for two reasons. Firstly, I don't like handing over control to other parties, particularly in relation to an ever-changing technical goalpost. Secondly, in terms of cost it is quite literally a bottomless pit, requiring never-ending investment and commitment. It seems to me that no sooner have you achieved the objective of getting into the top few on the rankings list than somebody else with a better IT genius or more cash overtakes you.

2 Google ad words and pay per click

If you can do it, then in my opinion this is much better. For those of you who aren't familiar with this concept, take a look at the rankings on the right-hand side of a Google search page and you will see what Google ad words is all about.

Providing you learn how to play this game or outsource your requirements, you have the opportunity to attract only relevant traffic to your website by effectively sponsored keywords. At its simplest, Google ad words enables you to produce visitors to your site who fit a certain profile, have particular interests or problems and are based in a specific geographical location. As pay per click might indicate, the great thing about this solution is that you only pay for actual visitors to your site.

The key of course is understanding how keywords work and what people actually search for. Be careful, however, because the most obvious words might produce visitors who have no interest in what you do. For example, including the word 'cruise' could easily produce visitors looking for cruise clothes or Tom Cruise the actor as opposed to your cruising travel agency, which you are seeking to promote.

3 Social media

We have already dealt with social media in this chapter, so let me simply reinforce the message. Participating on social media networks is a great free way to encourage people to visit your website. If you are not using social media opportunities to promote yourself or your business, you are potentially handing chunks of revenue – that should be yours – to your competition.

What are the most common traps in using the online world?

Forgetting there is an offline world

I have come across some 'technology' gurus who tell the business community to forget everything they have ever learned about business development and marketing communications and to direct every scrap of their efforts and resources into the online world. I fundamentally disagree with this approach and have one word I want readers of this book to take on board … 'integration'. What you need to be doing is taking advantage of the momentous and almost miraculous potential of the online world to develop your business, *but* in a way that enhances and fits in with other things you are already doing which work. Having all your eggs in one business development basket is not the best bet.

Failing to keep up the momentum and lack of patience

I have encountered many businesses that dive in with huge amounts of time and effort, highly excited by the potential of the online world, only to lose interest when results aren't instant. Don't be influenced by the miracle claims that you can read on the web every day, which tell you how one man and his dog made £1 million in the first few weeks of internet business development. Even if some of these claims are true, it is not the norm.

You should know and expect to have to work hard, sustain the momentum and anticipate that it is likely to be at least six months before you see sustained development, growth and success.

Spending too much time on the internet

I have come across a number of business people who get so hooked and addicted to being on the internet that they actually take their eye off the business ball. By all means invest time on the internet but don't enjoy it too much. After all, it is just another business and communications tool.

Not having a plan

I've encountered many businesses which proudly tell me how great they are doing online. When pressed for examples they tell me they have sent out a couple of e-mails to their customer base, joined a LinkedIn group and have a website. These are the 'techno dabblers' mentioned earlier.

The bottom line is this. If you are going to be successful online, you need a coherent and coordinated plan, so that your efforts are sustained and fit into other aspects of your business development. If you haven't got such a plan, then get one.

Not being selective

You don't have to use Twitter, Facebook and LinkedIn as if these activities were an online triathlon Olympic event. Choose your media and be selective. If you were going to buy paid advertising you wouldn't necessarily advertise with the same message in every single newspaper. Spread your time and energies. Make sure you match your business targets to the profile of your chosen media. If you are a business consultant selling to other businesses, then LinkedIn is likely to be more appropriate than Facebook, for example.

14 ways to develop your business through joint ventures and collaboration

Many businesses permanently beat themselves up with the question: what shall we do to generate more profitable customers and clients? I want to urge you to consider a different question, which has the potential to help you achieve your business development objectives much quicker, at a fraction of the cost and sometimes with little or no risk. The question you should therefore be asking is: **Who can we collaborate with to mutual benefit?**

Regardless of your size, joint venturing and commercial collaborations are without question one of the most underestimated yet most influential and effective ways of generating more leads and enquiries. In fact, for the smaller and even new business, these methods are absolutely appropriate and definitely not something to be ignored.

Let's begin with a great example of joint venturing and collaboration in action to show you what I mean.

Despite many changes in recent years and the ongoing shake up in the way legal services are provided, it is still a justifiable fact that to many the legal profession conjures up an image of stuffiness, inaccessibility, mystique, poor communications and value.

All this is changing, however, with the emergence of a number of new legal 'brands', setting out to get a significant market share of legal business, by creating a fresh and more accessible legal world driven by modern and dynamic concepts of 'customer service'.

At the time of writing the clear leader in the field is an organisation called QualitySolicitors, which has set out to become the Specsavers of the legal services sector ... and it is already well on its way.

What is of most interest, however, from a business development perspective, is the way much of what the company has already achieved is through the clever use of joint venturing and commercial collaborations.

Chief executive, Craig Holt, has brilliantly orchestrated several joint ventures, which include among other things:

■ getting law firms in different locations to collaborate as part of a national brand;

■ persuading high street retailer WH Smith to collaborate with QualitySolicitors, thus giving the legal brand what it calls 'Legal Access Points' in approximately 150 WH Smith stores around the country;

■ the establishment of deals with many other well-known consumer brands that provide discounts to the holders of QualitySolicitors' 'Legal Privilege Cards' that people can sign up to in WH Smith stores.

No doubt other such collaborations are on the way but this is a masterclass in joint-venture business development collaboration.

As a direct result of these arrangements, QualitySolicitors has in a very short space of time established a highly visible nationwide presence on our high streets; obtained massive promotional coverage; associated itself with an existing trusted name and brand; and, of course, created for itself a fantastic lead-generation system.

All very impressive, but what is the strategy behind Craig Holt's thinking in terms of business joint venturing? Does he have any golden rules for putting successful collaborations in place?

Craig Holt advises the following key things to strive for:

■ *'Collaborations that reflect the brand values of both parties.'*

■ *'Collaborations that give both parties demonstrable collective benefits and that would be difficult to achieve individually.'*

■ *'Not to be afraid of making approaches to organisations that are perceived as having a stronger brand than yours.'*

Most information about joint ventures perpetuates the common image that it is all about detailed legal agreements, pages of small print and lawyers and accountants thrashing out a very formal and complex deal. While I don't want to minimise the need to have a proper commercial understanding with those you might joint venture with, the truth is, many collaborations can be done relatively informally, quickly and are limited only by your commercial creativity and your willingness to make approaches and ask.

In essence a joint-venture collaboration is no more than two or more parties joining forces in some way to bring something different and of mutual benefit to the parties. I absolutely encourage all businesses, at the very least, to explore this possibility. If you are not joint venturing or considering collaborations then you are potentially missing out.

The tangible benefits of joint venturing include the following:

- getting into different customer and client bases;
- potentially massive cost savings;
- the endorsement factor ... working with a bigger brand than yours operates as an explicit endorsement of you;
- limitation and sharing of risks;
- information, experience and intelligence sharing.

All of these add up to one massive major benefit ... enhanced business development resulting in more customers, clients and profits.

So with this concept and these benefits in mind, let me give you 14 examples of various types of joint-venture collaboration. Of course this list is not exhaustive and some of them may be totally inappropriate to your business.

This list is simply meant to illustrate the range of possibilities and the contrast in scale and level of them, in order to act as a catalyst for your own business collaborative creativity. As you look through it, note how collaborations can take many forms, some of which you will have seen before but perhaps not really thought of as a business development collaborative tool:

1 Web links. The process of arranging reciprocal links between websites is a very simple form of joint venturing.

2 Getting newspapers and magazines to offer your products or services as special reader offers. For example, check out your weekend papers and you will see *The Times* travel offers or wine deals. Approach your local papers with similar arrangements.

3 Getting newspapers and magazines to offer publication-branded information guides. For example, I have in the past negotiated and

set up a 'Yorkshire Post Guide to Beating the Recession', between the *Yorkshire Post* and an accountancy firm.

4 The sharing of e-mails and databases. Subject to data protection legislation and privacy regulations, many businesses simply swap, buy and sell their respective databases.

5 Sponsorships. These can range from the huge mega brands sponsoring various events and causes, right down to a small business which invests £75 to sponsor a trophy given as an annual award at a prestigious regional drama festival.

6 Competitions. When the TV or newspapers run a competition and give away a prize, this has often been donated as part of a joint-venture collaboration.

7 Commission or royalty-based arrangements. These are extremely common and easy to set up. You simply find others in related areas who have a customer base of their own, who will market your goods or services to them. You pay commission to them on sales. You can also do this online through 'affiliate marketing'. Using this method you can potentially generate a huge number of additional leads.

8 Joint-venture seminars and events. I regularly get invited to seminars and events hosted and organised by two parties as part of a joint venture.

9 Speaking engagements. If you are offering a service and are able to talk knowledgeably about your various products then you could offer your speaking services at appropriate events. When an audience perceives you as the expert you are effectively showcasing your goods and services and driving business in your direction. The joint venture is with the organisers of the event, who are effectively endorsing and promoting you.

10 Joint branding deals. The AA now sells wills. Does this mean its car mechanics are out in their yellow vans providing legal services as well as fixing cars? No, of course not. It simply markets the service under its brand name, leveraging its client and customer base to harvest the business, which it then outsources to an appropriate legal practice. The two parties have a commercial arrangement.

11 Premises sharing. Visit a large department store and take a walk around the fashion departments. You will find a whole variety of fashion brands almost operating as a store within a store. If you have premises where you trade from, and space available, consider bringing in others as part of a joint venture.

12 Swapping people. You may have individuals with particular experience whom you can put into other organisations in exchange for them doing the same for you.

13 Trading services. Many businesses will be open to this. If you need a new website built and designed, perhaps a website design business will be open to you providing them with goods or services of appropriate value in exchange.

14 Use of gift certificates or vouchers. Let's suppose you run a restaurant, you could create some certificates or promotional offer vouchers, which you perhaps pass on to other businesses in the area to give to their customers as a gift or service-related gesture. When the gift or offer is taken up, an agreed payment is made to the distributing business.

It is quite clear from the above that joint collaborative ventures can take many forms and are absolutely appropriate to businesses of all sizes. I am often asked how you set up and establish such collaborations. The answer is very simple and always the same … you ask. It really is as simple as contacting another party and saying something along the lines of: *'Hi, my name is Bob Anderson. I'm one of the owners of the Italian restaurant on the high street and I've got a couple of ideas for joint promotional ventures that could be good for both of us. Are you up for a speculative chat?'* Rarely will such an invitation be turned down on the spot. Usually you will either meet, have a more detailed discussion over the phone or be asked to put your ideas in writing.

The absolute bottom line, however, is to make sure that as an integral part of your business development thinking you make a conscious effort to ask yourselves the question that I mentioned at the beginning: who can we collaborate with to mutual benefit?

How to win in competitive situations

If you are involved in business development, then there will almost certainly be times when you have the opportunity to formally compete and 'pitch' against other businesses to win a potential contract.

You may have the opportunity to submit a proposal, which will then be considered alongside those prepared by other, equally optimistic, competing businesses. Sometimes this will be as part of a formal tender process, where specific businesses have been approached to pitch for work.

This section takes a pragmatic and commonsense look at how to win competitively from my perspective as someone who has helped many businesses win millions of pounds worth of work in these sorts of situations.

As regards formal tenders, before going any further I want to mention that there are two types of tenders: private and public. Private tenders are those that are not driven by publicly funded bodies and organisations. In this book my focus is on private tenders or other more informal competitive business situations. This is simply because public sector tendering is very highly regulated by a massive amount of constantly changing and complex EU public procurement legislation, which is extremely political and involves constant red tape and hoop jumping. In terms of winning such a tender it is almost always driven by price-related factors and unless you are the cheapest your chances of success are more limited.

Despite these negatives, the fact is that there are a huge number of public sector opportunities for businesses out there. If you want to check them out, visit the relevant EU website: www.ted.europa.eu

I have personally been involved in supporting businesses in private sector tenders on over 100 occasions and have been fortunate to have a high win rate, resulting in millions of pounds worth of revenue for the businesses I have helped.

The reason I'm telling you this is simply so that you understand where the tips and traps below come from. They are not based on any academic or theoretical principles, but on real experience of observing and participating in many actual situations. The truth is, most businesses which don't perform well in tenders fall into the same few traps, whereas those organisations which consistently get good results tend to observe certain very simple rules. With this in mind here are the questions and issues I will be addressing:

■ How do these tender or other competitive opportunities arise?

■ Shall we go for it?

■ What are the six golden rules of winning?

■ What are the major traps?

■ How should the proposal be set out?

How do these tender or other competitive opportunities arise?

By invitation

Probably a third of the tender situations I am involved in are as a result of a direct approach by a company literally having pre-selected a business as a possible supplier and offering it the opportunity to tender. At that stage, you as a business would be sent what's usually known as an ITT (invitation to tender). This document, which can be of any length, will set out the opportunity and describe the tender process in detail.

Direct approaches

Other tender or competitive situations that frequently arise are as a direct result of prospecting, relationship building, networking both online and offline and by direct approaches to an organisation. Over the years I have had a lot of success on behalf of businesses making direct approaches, by asking an organisation when it is next going to be reviewing the suppliers of certain goods or services.

In one project 22 organisations were approached directly; nine told us that they were going to be reviewing over the next 18 months and then as a result of ongoing and structured contact, my client participated in four formal tenders and won three of them. One of them was worth £1.5 million in revenue per year! If you are not doing this, you may be missing out.

Existing clients

The other tender situations that arise quite frequently and which seem to be on the increase are those involving businesses which invite their existing suppliers to tender to retain their contract. This can be very frustrating for the incumbent supplier.

Many businesses putting forward such proposals often make the mistake of drafting the proposal and submitting it exactly as they would if they didn't know the client in the first place. The secret of success in these situations, however, is in drafting the proposal in such a way that it documents the gains that the company has had by using you, as well as the ongoing benefits of continuing to use you.

Shall we go for it?

Imagine the scenario. You receive an e-mail or letter out of the blue from a senior person in an organisation you have been communicating with for some time. They tell you that they are putting a particular job or project out to tender and ask whether you would like to express interest in participating in the tender process. As a business you now have a decision to make … shall we go for it or not? Here are a few tips to bear in mind:

Experience/expertise

You need to be absolutely scrupulously honest with yourselves over this. If you do not have the specific expertise or experience to deliver what is being asked then it is probably sensible to pass on the opportunity.

Resources

It may well be that you do have the experience and expertise but the scale of the project may be beyond your current resources. If you don't have the necessary resources and would not be prepared to take on the risks of investing in getting them, then again don't bother to participate.

Is it worth it?

I have seen a huge number of firms automatically tender for everything that they have the opportunity to go for. Don't be seduced by every business opportunity. You need to take a hard look at not just whether you could win it, but how profitable the contract might be in the future. I have experience of working with businesses which have been very smug that they have won tender contracts despite the fact that servicing them is unprofitable.

Don't make assumptions

Too many businesses assume that they have no chance for various reasons and then withdraw from the process. This can be a serious error of judgement.

If you do have the experience and expertise, the resources and you believe the potential business to be profitable, then go for it. Don't assume that you are too small, too big, or that other businesses have a much better chance and then back out on these grounds.

I have worked with organisations that have hesitated, but then gone for it and despite their initial negative assumptions have got contracts worth over £1 million.

What are the six golden rules of winning?

1 Be bold and find out more information about what is required

Never ever submit anything in writing to your prospect until you have tried to speak to them to get further information. Do this in every situation unless the ITT document specifically forbids you to do so.

There are three possibilities.

- Firstly, the invitation to tender will openly offer you the opportunity to speak to somebody to get more information. If this is the case, don't treat the offer as optional, regard it as mandatory and call for more information.

- Secondly, the invitation to tender document may be silent as regards gathering and providing more information. In this situation again make contact with the relevant person and ask how best to go about gathering what you need.

- Thirdly, you may find that contact and the opportunity to ask for more information is forbidden. In this instance you obviously observe this and don't ask.

The purpose of you making contact with the prospect after receiving the ITT is fairly obvious. Your aim is to be able to engage them in conversation, where you get valuable nuggets of information that you can use and that your competitors won't have, because they haven't bothered to ask.

So, what should you ask? First of all make sure that you resist all temptations to turn any conversation into a sales pitch. You need to focus on asking questions in a conversational style in order to draw out as much information as possible.

Don't be afraid of asking commercially sensitive questions, such as: why are you putting this out to tender?; who have you been using in the past?; what sort of problems and issues have you faced?; what sort of fee or price structure would be within your ballpark?; who will make the decisions, and what criteria will they use in their final choice?

It is also important that in asking these questions you do so in a way that makes it easy for the other party to decline to answer, without feeling uncomfortable. For example: *'Forgive me if this is a bit too commercially sensitive, but it would be really helpful in checking if there is a good fit. Are you able to share the kind of pricing structure that you have in mind?'*

2 Focus on them

Too many proposals begin with a rambling outline of a company's history and background and a whole host of irrelevant facts and figures about the organisation. This is often followed up with nothing more than a list of the various services and products offered.

Your prospect is not really interested in you or your business, other than what benefits you can bring to them. It is vital, therefore, that in writing your proposal you refer to them a lot and specifically to their requirements and how what you have to offer will benefit them.

3 Establish credibility

When the prospects read through the various proposals they know that it is a promotional document and that all tendering organisations will 'puff' themselves up to make themselves sound fantastic. The proposals that consistently do well are those that give proof statements to add credibility to any claims made. So, for example, if you are claiming substantial experience give actual figures to illustrate. Explain how many years, how many customers, track record of results, etc.

Don't just talk about quality of service provided, actually include testimonials from satisfied customers. Purely by way of example here is one I recently received with regard to a tender I worked on for an organisation:

> 'Ian, We just wanted to say a big thanks for the help and support on our recent tender, which as you now know was successful. Your guidance, advice, drafting support and overall contribution played a significant part in ensuring that we won this tender. This was a big and very important piece of business for the firm and your involvement was an integral part in the success of our bid.'

So, go out and ask for testimonials.

4 Keep in mind who you are writing the tender for

If you're writing a proposal as part of a competitive process, ask yourself this vital question: who am I writing this for? The temptation of course is to give the obvious answer, which is the company or business that has invited tenders. In practice, however, that is not the case. The correct answer is the specific individual that you need to influence who will have the biggest say in any decision-making.

Therefore it is important to try to find out who the decision-making person or people will be and then to do as much homework as possible to find out whatever you can about them and their preferred style.

5 Have a summary of benefits

I was asked by a director of a business to read through a proposal document his organisation had just prepared and to give him some feedback. Having read the document, my question was: what are the most compelling reasons why you as a business should be chosen? He told me that this information was in the proposal. Indeed it was, but to find these reasons I had to wade through 41 pages of text.

With this in mind make sure that on the first page of any competitive proposal you write, you have a summary of benefits so that whoever is reading it is able instantly to see what the most powerful reasons are. Make sure this summary is not more than two pages, has clear headings and lots of space to emphasise the elements you want to be seen.

6 Get feedback after the process

Win or lose, make sure that you do everything you possibly can to try to find out in detail how your proposal was perceived.

If you were successful then you need to try to find out which elements of your proposal had the most influence. If you were not, then you need to understand what else you could have done.

What are the major traps?

Failure to differentiate from the competition

Too many businesses simply provide factual information about themselves and give a low price. This gives the prospect the challenge of working out for themselves why they should choose your business. If there is nothing to differentiate you from your competitors other than price then you either won't win the contract or you will but for the wrong reasons and regret it later.

Failure to tailor the proposal

Many organisations take the easy way out when it comes to preparing proposals. They immediately dive into the computer and pull up proposals that they may have written in the past, even if they have been unsuccessful ones! They then use the 'find and replace' function on their computer to change a few names and facts here and there.

While there may be some generic material that can be adapted, you should assume that a very high percentage needs to be tailored to the very specific requirements of your prospect.

Not taking enough time

You should be under no illusions that drafting and crafting winning proposals will take time. There are no shortcuts. Decide to do it properly or don't do it at all.

Non-compliance

Most ITT documents will set out precisely what is required in the proposal as well as how it should be set out and submitted. You must observe these tender compliance issues absolutely or you risk being automatically ruled out for non-compliance. My advice on this is to prepare a detailed compliance checklist very early on in the process and tick each item off prior to submission.

How should the proposal be set out?

- Begin your proposal with a very brief introduction that summarises your understanding of the objectives and requirements and your enthusiasm to work with the organisation.

- Give your summary of benefits as mentioned in no more than one or two sides.

- Answer all questions, dealing with all issues that the organisation raises, using its language and phraseology wherever possible. Also use the headings and any numbering sequence that it uses.

- Include any examples, case studies and testimonials that you can, in order to illustrate the benefits your goods and services have brought others in the past.

- Include a conclusion that is short and to the point, which draws all your benefits together and provides a powerful assurance of your confidence.

Brand your way to business development success

We live in the 'brands age'. Everywhere we look we are surrounded by business, product or personal brands. Make no mistake, however cynical about them you might be, in the absence of specific business recommendations or very strong past loyalties you will almost always end up buying from a known brand name.

With this in mind, if you want to develop your business, then it is clearly a massive advantage to be able to develop a brand. By the way, having a small business or providing a personal service under your own name is no barrier. It is still perfectly possible and indeed desirable to establish a brand around you or your enterprise. Good branding can and will drive potential customers and clients into your 'enquiries and leads bucket'.

Research the subject of branding and you will encounter a huge amount of academic waffle. For example, my own reading on the subject brought up this little gem that talks about branding, *'as a supporting theoretical framework that postulates a differential brand message'* and goes on to *'discuss the historical setting of branding and the link to linguistic paradigms'*. This unnecessarily complicates the topic.

On the other hand there are those folk who take an oversimplistic approach and say all you need to do to create a brand is get a decent logo. Hence, I have seen many organisations decide to go through a branding or re-branding exercise and simply change their name, design colour or logo.

If you had an unsuccessful business before, then if all you do is change the name and symbol, the likelihood is you will have an unsuccessful business in the future but with a glossy new logo that has cost you money to get designed.

So with this in mind let's get real and practical.

Your brand is essentially what people say about your business when you are not listening

If they don't know who you are at all, or if what they say about you is not what you would like them to be saying or feeling, then you either don't have a brand or you have one that is not doing the job. Think about this carefully. The creation of your brand and what it conveys is absolutely within your control and there are a number of things that you can do to build a strong brand in order to have the level of influence that you want in the market place.

What word or adjective immediately jumps into your mind at the mention of the following brands? Apple, Rolls-Royce, Skoda, Poundstretcher, Rolex, Timex, John Lewis, The Financial Times, Primark, Harrods. The phrases that immediately spring to your mind represent the brand message behind these operations.

Five ways to 'BRAND'™ whatever you are selling

If you want to establish a strong brand, then the issues that you must address can be remembered by my acronym BRAND. Here is what it stands for and the things you need to strive to do. The more of these you can achieve the better.

B = Bold positioning statement

Have a bold statement about yourself and make sure you constantly reinforce it very openly and uniformly in all your external and internal communications. It might even be in your promotional information or in your strap-line.

In the early part of the book I mentioned Viking River Cruises that has the strapline 'the world's leading river cruise line… by far'. With this message constantly repeated in everything it does and alongside its logo, it no longer becomes mere promotion but almost a statement of fact that gets into the consciousness of existing customers, prospects and staff.

R = Realism

Your brand message must reflect reality and honesty. The worst thing you can do is to position yourself as one thing when it is demonstrably obvious to all that this is not the case. Thus positioning yourself at the premium end of your market as a luxury and high-quality supplier is pointless if the goods and services you offer are incredibly cheap and poor.

A = Association

What 'mental association' do people have with your brand name? What is the 'feeling' the name or brand gives the moment you see or hear the name? Is it luxury or value; great service or style; reassurance and comfort?

Having made that decision you need to ensure that all business development initiatives are in line with that thinking in a very real and practical way. This then should influence your decisions and actions on recruitment, design, levels of service, quality control, operational functions and pricing.

You should also know that your brand is the sum of the associations and experiences that people have had and heard, relating to your business. With this in mind, make sure they are good ones!

N = Name awareness

You have to take steps to ensure your target market instantly knows your business name. Your name needs to be out there in as many relevant places as possible. It needs to be visible and frequently seen, and encountered by your potential prospects and targets.

That is why merely focusing on one medium is not enough. Have an integrated approach so that your name and brand identity are used both online and offline. Ideally your prospects should be seeing your name pop up wherever they go in a variety of different contexts.

> For example, I have previously mentioned a new brand in the legal market place... QualitySolicitors. This morning I read a discussion about it on a LinkedIn group; yesterday I saw an interview on television about it; and when I picked up my news-paper over the weekend the first thing I saw was a large advertisement. If that wasn't enough a few days later I walked into WH Smith to buy a bar of chocolate and guess who had a presence in the store offering me information?
>
> This gives a sense of familiarity with the firm and begins to establish it in my con-sciousness as a major trusted player and prospective supplier of legal services. As mentioned earlier, in the absence of a strong, personal, past relationship, with this level of branding there is every chance that QualitySolicitors would get onto my mental shopping list next time I need some legal support.

D = Distinctiveness

Regardless of whether it is a product, a business name or even an indi-vidual, it helps branding if it can be associated with some very distinctive or memorable image. This might be a logo, a name style or even a personal photograph or something that makes the image instantly recognisable within your target market. If I were to show you just logos and even 'house colours' of some leading brands you would immediately be able to mention the name or product and in turn that would trigger the adjective or 'asso-ciation' mentioned earlier. For example, if I were to show you the colour purple and ask you to think of a brand of chocolate, what name would pop into your head? I'll bet you can even taste it, just from the mere thought right now.

If there is nothing visibly distinctive about you or your business at the moment, create something and use it often. Being distinctive and memo-rable is important in any branding exercise.

Jonathan Straight, chief executive of Straight plc, the UK's leading supplier of waste and recycling containers, claims:

'I did it with a waxed moustache and hundreds of pairs of spectacles. The commercial world can be grey and boring. Make sure you stand out and you are noticed.'

Direct targeting by telephone

Despite all the wonders of the internet and social media business development revolution, there are still many businesses out there producing significant results by directly targeting via the telephone. Yes ... telesales. It might be seen as dated and generally unpopular but I still see this work very well in certain circumstances. There is an elegant simplicity in calling up prospects very openly and asking them if they would like to do business.

My own personal view is that in the volume-driven business to consumer (B2C) market, telesales is a highly labour-intensive method with a high level of wastage and poor proportionate return. Where I still see good results, however, is in the B2B world where organisations are sensible enough to cherry pick specific businesses to approach.

Here are a few tips, traps and general comments to take on board if you are considering this activity.

Be very selective

Only decide to use this strategy if you can produce a list of business targets that you absolutely know for sure need your goods or services.

> For example, if you are in the cleaning business and specialise in the hotels, guest-houses and residential care homes sector in a particular city, then this kind of approach can work well if done properly. It absolutely makes sense simply to produce a list of very relevant target establishments and make direct contact with them with a view to doing business.

Go for quality not quantity

Some years ago I heard a telesales trainer ask his audience, 'If you get four appointments having telephoned 100 targets, how many targets do you have to call in order to get eight appointments?' His answer was 200. He then told his delegates that the secret was to 'double your failure rate'. What absolute nonsense.

Surely, the best strategy and aim is to improve the quality of the approach and of the target base in order to double your *success* rate.

Should you send a letter before calling?

My own preference is not to do this. I have rarely seen any real benefit, despite the logical arguments often put forward in favour of this approach. If you feel you must, however, then make sure it is a really good and well-written letter from a business development copywriting point of view. (See the writing skills section in Chapter 8.)

The other thing you must do is to make sure that you follow it up quickly. There is no point in waiting three weeks and then making a telephone call referring to it.

Turn your target list into a league table before calling

Before you make any calls, organise the list of your targets so that your most desirable prospect is right at the top and you have the rest in rank order. You should then start making the calls from the bottom upwards. This way you have the opportunity to develop the most effective content, structure and style before you get to the juiciest possibilities.

Get great strikers

One of the great problems with telesales campaigns is the perception that anyone can do it. It is not unusual for organisations to bring in inexperienced, lowly paid, part-time people and have them ring as many people as they can on the list and quite literally read out a script. This strategy is rarely going to produce great results.

If you want to maximise the business development potential of this technique then make sure you have got some strikers. These are people who are seriously committed and professional. Working around a central theme driven by your objectives they are literally able to call your carefully selected target list and engage prospects in a conversation. With this in mind, if you are tempted by telesales then make sure you have the right people in place to do it for you.

Do not use fixed scripts

How often have you heard people who call you simply reading from a script? The great problem with having a totally inflexible script written out for telesales people to read is that the people you are calling don't have their bit written out as well. The truth is, it is impossible to script a real conversation and unless you are having a proper dialogue, your chances of success are massively reduced.

Let me be provocative. If the people you are engaging to make your calls for you aren't bright enough to do so without a script, don't use them at all. While I absolutely do not believe in fixed scripts, however, I do believe in having a prepared structure that your caller is able to steer people through.

Do not lie

How many times have you heard callers give you the *'I'm not trying to sell you anything'* line? They know it's a lie and so do you. I hardly think they are ringing 1,000 strangers to chat about their health. The call may be dressed up as a survey, or information about a competition, but we all know it is part of a sales process.

If you want to be successful with telesales, or indeed any kind of sales, then don't lie. How much respect and trust is going to be communicated if the opening line of the sales approach is a blatant fib?

Be open and use the PARA approach to calling

I obviously can't tell you what you should say relating to your business, but let me give you some guidance on the general approach that I have seen produce excellent results. To understand and remember this approach and structure, think of the acronym PARA.

P = Pre-frame

Pre-framing is a simple linguistic technique, where you tell someone at the beginning what is to come and sometimes how to react. This operates as a softener or as a way of removing objections before they arise. For example, by recognising very early on in the call that you are aware that the business you are calling is almost certain to have an existing supplier of the goods and services you sell, it immediately shows your understanding of the sector and removes that most obvious objection.

A = Aligning

This is the process of saying something that shows you absolutely understand how your call is likely to be received from the recipient's point of view. For example: *'I really appreciate you taking my call, because I know when it's the other way around how frustrating it can be taking sales calls totally out of the blue.'*

R = Review

If you have been smart in your selection of a target list then all the businesses you ring ought to have an ongoing requirement for your type of goods and services. It therefore becomes a very valid question on the back of pre-framing and aligning to politely ask a question along the lines of: *'As I said, I know the likelihood is that you have an existing supplier, but I wonder if you would mind sharing with me if and when you will be reviewing contracts?'*

A = Action

Whatever the outcome of the call, take some action. If you have promised to send the recipient some information, then keep your promise. This might sound like a statement of the obvious, but keep in mind some past research I did which revealed that only 50 per cent of organisations which promised to send follow-up information actually kept their promise.

Avoid the gatekeeper problems

Whenever the subject of telesales comes up, I always get asked the question: 'What's the best way of dealing with the gatekeepers?' There are whole books written on this subject, so if you are really interested by all means dip into them. Let me save you a lot of bother, however, by cutting straight to the chase. **Do not lie, trick or manipulate your way past them**.

I have found the best approach is to be as totally open and friendly as possible. Share with them what you want and even ask them the best way forward with their organisation. You will be pleasantly surprised (if not a bit shocked) at just how much information you may get from a gatekeeper.

No doesn't mean never

The head of marketing at a particular client company told me recently, *'There's no point in targeting property developers in the region because we did that and they all said no.'* When I asked when these approaches had been made I was told, *'Almost three years ago.'*

Just because you have had 'no' in the past, it doesn't mean you will get a 'no' for ever. The most important thing to bear in mind here is that things change. The people your business approached may now have left, the person who made the call may now be different, your target's circumstances and requirements may have changed too. The message therefore is clear: be persistent.

Keep records

However many businesses you approach by telephone, keep detailed notes of who made the call, to whom, what was said and what was agreed in terms of action.

Re-define success

One of the biggest problems I encounter with this technique is that businesses automatically regard it as a failure if they don't come off the telephone with some business or at the very least an appointment.

If you feel like this, then I would like to take the pressure off you. You should regard the initial phone call as the first step of several contacts. In the B2B world it is the norm that several contacts will be required before you get a 'yes'. With this in mind, don't give up at the first hurdle.

Sometimes just gaining useful information should be regarded as a success.

8

Personal performance business development skills

Consider this for a moment. If you have never had a golf or tennis lesson and have limited natural aptitude, you wouldn't dream of participating in these sports at a competitive professional level. Yet this is precisely what many people do when it comes to business. They will go out into the very competitive business world hoping to win, with no training or guidance, determined to get great results, without having the basic personal business development skills that they need to be effective. Strategy without skills is ineffective.

It is simple common sense that, even if you know what to do, if you or your team don't have what I call the necessary 'personal performance business development skills', don't expect great business development results.

I have identified the six key skill areas and created a very simple device and tool to assess you and your people.

Personal performance skills score sheet

With 10 being outstanding and 1 being poor, how would you rate yourself and your individual team members and employees in the skill areas in the box overleaf? Get them all to do this also for themselves and then compare the results.

Taking into account your scoring of your team and team members for themselves, an average of less than 40 points out of 60 and your people really need to consider extra training. Under 30 points and your business development results will be absolutely massively affected. Do not spend another penny on external activities until you have started to fix this.

Skill area	Score
Sales skills	_____
Writing skills	_____
Conversational business networking skills	_____
Presentation/public speaking skills	_____
Negotiation skills	_____
Time management skills	_____

Sales skills and tips

Selling is the art of using conversational questions in order to help a buyer get what they need or want at a price that is profitable for you and makes them feel good enough to want to come back for more.

Selling is not:

- telling prospects how great you or your products are;
- hard persuasion or pressure;
- putting a stupidly cheap price on something;
- using manipulative tricks, telling lies or massaging the truth to get someone to buy.

Understand the sales staircase

Be patient, you don't always have to open and close the deal during the first contact with the customer. The best sales people understand that patience is a virtue. See the process as a staircase with each contact leading you upwards towards the next step and, of course, your goal. Indeed it is not uncommon in B2B sales to have seven or more interactions or contacts before a sale is actually made. Inexperienced or impatient sales people often give up after the first two or three.

Use questions to identify problems and concerns

Instead of merely 'tell selling', where you simply tell the prospect how great you or your products are, the best sales people have a different strategy. They use conversational and rapport-building questions to get the prospect talking about why they are potentially interested in making a purchase.

With the right questions a prospect will usually share the problems and concerns they have, that have brought them to you. Skilful sales people know it is important to go through this process so that the prospect will eventually take ownership of the solution that you offer.

Ask the magic 'Would it be helpful?' question

Would it be helpful to learn a killer sales question? I'm always hesitant about giving particular phrases or scripts to people in sales situations but this one works more often than not.

Once you have your potential customer or client at the stage where they are sharing their problems and concerns, you could consider this 'magic' question. So for example:

■ Would it be helpful to fix up an appointment?

■ Would it be helpful if I show you a bigger model?

■ Would it be helpful if we can work out a special deal for you?

■ Would it be helpful if we can deliver that within your timescale?

■ Would it be helpful if we can come up with something to solve that problem for you at a sensible price?

Providing you don't ask this too early, you will get a 'yes' most of the time. How did you mentally answer the opening question at the beginning of this tip?

Ask for what you want outright

I have witnessed and experienced this thousands of times. One of the biggest sales traps of all, when people conclude the sales conversation or contact, is not asking outright for what they really want. For example, don't 'if' the prospect away. Whatever you do, don't end your conversation with, *'So if you'd like to go ahead, please don't hesitate to get back in touch with us.'* The moment you use the word 'if', you are implicitly pushing the prospect away, sowing seeds of doubt in their mind and losing control of the situation. So without hesitancy or being over-pushy, ask something like:

■ *'May I take it you'd like to go ahead?'*

■ *'When is it convenient to get together to take this further?'*

Ask choice questions

Sometimes when asking for what you want you can get a better result by asking the question and then offering two choices with specific positive alternative answers. So for example instead of saying, *'Would you like to make an appointment?'*, you might ask instead, *'Based on what you have just told me, it strikes me the best way of taking this forward is for us to get together. When is most convenient for you? How about either the 12th or 15th of October?'* This takes the prospect into what I call diary mode, where they are now focusing on which date is best for them, rather than on both the positives and negatives of going ahead at all.

Share your confidence in your products or services and your desire to have them

Customers want to feel good about the purchase they are making. If you have built appropriate rapport with them, identified the problems and concerns and shown there is a 'fit' between what you have to offer and their requirement, then telling them, *'I am absolutely 100 per cent confident that we can really help you sort those problems out and we would love to have you as a customer'*, or words to that effect, will really oil the wheels of the potential sale. Make sure, however, you really mean it and are able to say it sincerely.

Learn to overcome objections

There are whole books and expensive courses on this issue alone. Many sales people actually fear asking for the business or seeking feedback because they are worried that the prospect will have an objection. Here are a few commonsense tips on dealing with objections.

Don't argue

I have come across many sales people who think that the way to overcome the objection is to argue and be confrontational with the prospect. If a potential customer or client says, *'I'm sorry, you're just too expensive'*, don't respond with, *'No we're not, we like to think we're pretty competitive, we know of many others who are much more expensive than us.'* As a basic rule you're not going to get a great result by taking an opposing argumentative position.

Don't panic and start 'tell selling'

Some sales people deal with objections by being panicked into an outpouring of breathless benefits about their products or services. This will, in most cases, not help.

Don't justify on the grounds that it is good for you

Believe it or not I have heard sales people say, *'Oh come on, I need to meet my sales targets this month.'*

Plan for specific objections in advance

Some people deal with objections as if they are surprised by them and have never heard them before. I guarantee that if I ask you to make a list of all the possible objections that might be raised, you will be hard pushed to raise more than five or six. What this means is that you can identify them in advance and then plan and discuss the best way of dealing with each of them.

Use questions to overcome objections

There are several techniques that really work. Let me give you a few examples.

Ask SSOD IT™ questions. This is an acronym device of mine and stands for:

S = Sow
S = Seeds
O = Of
D = Doubt

SSOD IT is basically the technique of first aligning with your prospect and then asking a couple of questions that sow seeds of doubt in their mind. When you then ask them to reconsider the proposition, they do so with these doubts firmly in their mind. For example, suppose you have a price objection ... you could say:

'You know what, I can totally understand you being hesitant given that we are a little more expensive than some (aligning) ... but let me ask you a couple of questions to help you decide once and for all. Will the other company you mentioned be able to deliver as quickly as ours within a specific time? Have you any idea who will actually be doing the job at the other firm and their level of experience, specialisation and track record? Let me reassure you by ... etc.'

What's happened here is that by saying you understand their position, you will align with them, which means you haven't threatened the rapport you should have built up, and by asking the various questions you get them to reconsider for themselves whether they are actually comparing like with like.

'If we were able to' questions

Regardless of the objection you could try asking this very simple question which almost always begins with 'if we were able to...'. For example:

- *'If we were able to come up with a better deal, would you be happy to go ahead?'*
- *'If we were able to do something about the delivery date, would you be happy to go ahead?'*
- *'If we were able to guarantee results, would that make you feel more comfortable?'*

Clearly, you need to tailor the exact question around their objection.

Ask what you would need to do to get the business

Sometimes it can pay to be upfront and ask the following very open question: *'We'd really love to have your business. Would you mind me asking precisely what we would have to do to make you feel comfortable about going ahead with us?'* Very often the prospect will tell you and sometimes you will be able to give them what they are looking for and sometimes not.

Quit after the first 'yes'

Now here is a real quirk. I have often experienced sales people carrying on selling and justifying after they have already got the 'yes' they wanted. They throw more into the pot and end up saying something that makes the prospect change their mind. Get the 'yes' you want and then shut up.

Writing skills and tips

Business development writing skills are about using the written word to influence the reaction or emotion of your customer as they read it. Here are a few practical commonsense tips.

Numbers have power

If you are trying to write influential and persuasive copy, bear in mind that numbers have power. For example, instead of simply saying 'We have experience in personal injury claims', a firm of solicitors might put 'We have 25 years' specialist experience in personal injury claims, helped over 61,000 people get the compensation they deserve and won over £26 million worth of compensation every year for the past five years.'

What is there about your products and services that you can turn into numbers?

Write conversationally

For some reason, something often happens to people when they sit down to write promotional or marketing material. They feel compelled to adopt a formal style and approach. Try to avoid this as much as possible. Write your material in the chatty and anecdotal way you would speak to someone. You want your reader to feel comfortable and that you really understand how they think and feel.

Focus on benefits and not just features

Let me explain the difference. A feature is usually some physical attribute of your goods or services and a benefit statement explains what the prospect will get out of this feature or the problem it solves.

Of course it's okay to list the features of your offerings, but do make sure that you include some benefits as well, so that it is clear that what you are selling meets the needs and wants of your prospects.

Use questions in your writing

Would you like to know the 21 magic words and phrases that most influence people to buy? How would you like to transform your written material into a cash machine?

If the answer to both of these questions is yes, then the demonstration has worked. What questions can you come up with in your own copy?

How much time will your readers spend reading your material?

If you are fortunate enough to get someone to your website or your glossy brochure into the hands of a prospect, how much time will they spend reading your material? If you estimate they will only spend 30 seconds, then why are you giving them 5 minutes worth?

With this in mind, you need to make sure that your key messages can be read and processed in a realistic time period.

Understand and try the name change test

Have a look at any promotional material, leaflets or indeed your website copy that has been written. Now cross out or change the name of your business or brand to that of a competitor's and read the material again. If it reads exactly the same and still works as a generic piece of copy, then you have a problem.

Any written material ought to be specific to your operation and target market.

Meet AIDA

This is a well-established acronym to help with copywriting. If you haven't already met it, then here it is. Check that all elements are present in your copy in this order:

A = **Attention.** The heading needs to be attention grabbing to make the reader stop.

I = **Interest.** The words that are used should be designed to focus on the likely problems and concerns that the reader might have. That is why the question techniques above are so important.

D = **Desire.** The words need to be chosen to actively make the reader want you or your products or service.

A = **Action.** Make sure that before you finish you have told your readers exactly what action they have to take and give them as few simple steps as possible.

21 magic copywriting words and phrases

Here are 21 powerful, easy to use and simple to learn, tried and tested phrases that are 100 per cent guaranteed to get you the quick results and dramatic difference you want.

The above sentence may be a little contrived in this context, but the words and phrases that carry huge influence include, among others:

1 You

2 Save

3 Improvement

4 Results

5 Confidence

6 Powerful

7 Easy to use

8 Simple to learn

9 Tried and tested

10 100 per cent guaranteed

11 Quick results

12 Dramatic difference

13 You want

14 Special offer

15 Free

16 How to

17 Bargain price

18 New

19 Limited time

20 Exclusive

21 Without risk

Consciously, see how you can work some of these phrases into your copy without overdoing it or being too contrived, like my sentence above.

Conversational networking skills and tips

I have addressed the power and influence of social media networking earlier on but this section looks at the basic old-fashioned skill of face-to-face conversation. The importance of it in business development should not be under-estimated. Here are a few tips.

Business networking opportunities are everywhere

Let me ask you a question. When was the last time you were in a business networking situation? If you have mentally started to list your breakfast networking meetings, trade shows, business seminars or events, you are absolutely missing the point.

The truth is business networking opportunities are quite literally everywhere. Business networking is simply about meeting people and developing and maintaining relationships with them. Don't miss the fact that business networking is not just a formal activity that you have to separate from the rest of your life. Your entire life is based around meeting people and the quality of relationships that you develop will influence how successful you are. Whether you are on holiday, travelling on a train or standing next to somebody in a queue, you are in a position to network all the time. Don't miss the opportunities that life throws at you.

At formal business social events most people feel like you

You should know that around 97 per cent of people going to business social events use words like 'apprehensive' or 'nervous' to describe how they feel. Remember this when you are looking around the room and everybody else seems to be having a wonderful time.

You don't need to push or do hard sell in business networking situations

I have often seen business people pushing their way through the crowds at a business event handing out brochures and their business cards like hungry predators treating other guests like prey.

Not only is this not a good strategy, it is positively counter-productive. With this in mind, do not think of business networking situations as a place to indulge in hard sell.

The whole purpose of these events is to build on relationships you have and to meet new people you can establish a rapport with. In the vast majority of situations it is unlikely that anyone is going to do business with you unless they like and trust you. You won't establish that relationship if you pitch to them within the first few seconds.

Small talk is big business

I am always asked, how do you move small talk to big talk and social to business? Here is the simple answer. In your early conversation in some form of networking situation, don't worry about it. Small talk is the process of finding something in common. It is the foreplay of a conversational relationship. Keep it simple and focus your interest on the person you are talking to rather than on yourself. However, as a starting point to moving things forward, make one of the small-talk conversations about them, their business role and their business. You will find things will flow from there. Remember, they are there to network just like you.

Learn the two golden rules of great conversation

The two most important tools of great conversation in any situation are:

1 just ask, and

2 just listen.

It is absolutely vital to understand that whoever asks the questions controls the conversation. Therefore if you want to become a great conversationalist and a good business networker you must first master the simple art of asking good conversational questions. The art of asking questions is to steer the conversation in the direction you want, always looking for common ground.

Having asked appropriate questions make sure you listen effectively to the responses. When you listen, be absolutely attentive with good eye contact and facial expressions and avoid looking around for others, checking your text messages or your watch when somebody is talking to you. People know when you are not really listening and apart from the fact that it is simply rude it won't help you develop a future business relationship.

Have a personal introduction

Here is a bizarre phenomenon. Despite the fact that you have been asked the *'What do you do?'* question thousands of times in all sorts of situations and will be asked many more times in the future, many people struggle to come up with a really good answer and even seem surprised by the question.

A good response is one that provokes further conversation and questions and one that conveys how you help others or, at the very least, indicates the area of your specialisation. Your answer can change according to who you are meeting, but most important of all is to make sure you have thought it through in advance and without hesitation are able to trot out something helpful when required. If you can, ask whoever you are talking to this same question first. Their answer might influence which response of yours you use!

Play conversational tennis

When someone asks you a question, don't just give one word answers. Give a proper response and always ask questions back. Good conversations usually involve turn taking. Each question and response leads to the likelihood of the two people establishing something in common.

For formal events, actively plan ahead with follow-up time

One of the biggest problems I encounter is with people not following up and keeping in touch with the people they have met. Here are a few tips for this:

- Create time in advance. If you know that you are attending a business networking event, actually build some follow-up time into your diary for the day or so after to decide and act on the next step.

- Follow up everybody you have met even if it is just with a quick courtesy e-mail.

- Don't just stuff cards into a drawer. Add all those you have met to your contacts system and decide on activity for the future.

- Actively consider how you can give support and help to the contacts you have made. Remember, people will be more inclined to help you if you do something for them first.

- Keep your promises. When you're talking to them, let them see you jot down any promises you make about getting in touch. When you do, start any communication with *'As promised...'*.

- Use social media networking. Integrate your face-to-face networking with any social media networking you do. Always check if the people that you have met face to face are on LinkedIn, Facebook, Twitter or other networks and then seek to connect with them.

'Be civil to all; sociable to many; familiar with few; friend to one; enemy to none.'
Benjamin Franklin

Presentation skills and tips

One trademark agent and scientist I had to train to present told me, *'I'd rather set fire to my legs than speak in public.'* A little extreme, but it is a fact that giving presentations is not everybody's cup of tea. Nevertheless the ability to be able to speak and influence groups of people is an important skill for those with a business development role.

Here then are a few brief and simple tips to observe.

Throw the rulebook away and be yourself

Many presentation trainers and books will give you a rigid set of rules. Some will say don't move your hands too much; that men should keep their jackets on, with buttons done up; don't move around; use visual aids, etc.

My tip is this. Chuck the fixed rulebook away and do what works for you. Be yourself. I have seen some of the best communicators and presenters in the world break all of the above rules and yet still hold an audience in the palm of their hands.

It's not what you say but how you say it

Think of your favourite comedian and their most popular routines. I absolutely guarantee you that if you had the script to their material and you delivered it to an audience, it would not be half as funny. The bottom line is that too many presenters focus only on the content and not on the tone and style of their delivery.

With this in mind, one of the most important tips I can give you is to be congruent. In other words, your tone and style of delivery must match what you are saying. I have seen many presenters get up and tell the audience, *'I'm so excited and delighted to be here.'* The only problem is that because they are saying this in a dull, unexcited monotone, with a miserable expression on their face, their comment loses any power and influence or credibility.

Remember who you are talking to

Never get up in front of an audience without asking yourself, *'Who is my audience?'* Your content, language, style and indeed everything about your presentation should be adapted and moulded to the profile of your audience.

Be there

Whatever time you have been given to do your presentation, aim if possible to be there at least an hour before and if you have to give an early-morning presentation, then if possible, go the night before.

Check everything

If your presentation involves visual aids, sound equipment, a lectern, etc. then checking and double-checking everything relating to your presentation is not being paranoid, it is, in fact, being professional.

Practise out loud

I have come across many people whose idea of practice and preparation is to mentally read through their presentation beforehand. This may make you more familiar with what you are going to do and say but it is not proper practice. Unless you actually get up somewhere and say what you are going to say out loud it doesn't count. Remember: presenting is an external process.

Understand the 'tell them three times' rule

There is a very simple and basic structure to help shape any presentation you give:

- Tell them what you are going to tell them.
- Tell them it.
- Tell them what you have just told them.

Learn and master the ICQES™ formula

This is a very simple acronym that I devised when training nervous presenters how to get into their presentations. Use it, in this order:

I = Introduction. Get up and in a totally congruent style simply greet your audience and give your name. For example: *'A very good morning ladies and gentlemen, my name is Ian Cooper and I'm the author of* The Financial Times Guide to Business Development.*'*

C = Credibility. This is when you very simply make sure the audience knows who you are and your credentials. For example: *'If you're wondering who I am to be speaking to you today, all you need to know is that for the past 27 years I have helped over 800 businesses generate millions of pounds worth of revenue and today I'm going to share some of these business development secrets with you.'*

Q = Questions. Now ask your audience three rhetorical questions as a platform for what you will be talking about later on. For example: *'Have you ever wondered what makes some business development activities more successful than others? What is the quickest and most foolproof way to win more profitable customers and clients? What is the first and most important thing you should be doing when you get back to the office? These are just some of the issues I will be addressing in this presentation.'*

E = Establish control. It is perfectly okay to feel a little nervous when you get up to speak. Giving an introduction, explaining your credentials and posing some questions gives you the chance to get yourself and your voice under control. Use this stage to tell the audience if you are going to take questions, about any handouts, if you are taking a break, etc. You need them to appreciate you are in control.

S = Structure. This is when you explain what you are going to tell them and how the presentation will unfold.

Coping with nerves

If you feel nervous before a presentation then there is a word that describes you … normal. Here are a few points to bear in mind and to help with this issue:

- *Alcohol* – avoid it before presenting.

- *Preparation* – thorough preparation on every aspect of your presentation is what should give you the peace of mind and confidence to be as relaxed as possible.

- *Sympathetic audience* – on the vast majority of occasions, your audience is not looking to catch you out and will be on your side.

- *Questions* – if you are going to take questions, make a list of all possible questions you think you might be asked in advance and prepare possible answers.

- *You are human* – have realistic expectations. The only person who expects you to be Superman or Superwoman is you!

- *Breathe deeply* – take plenty of calming deep breaths just before you get up to present.

Visual aids work for you and not the other way round

I'm always asked, *'Do I have to use visual aids such as PowerPoint or Keynote?'* The simple answer is *'No'*, you don't have to. The real question is, *'How will such visual aids enhance my presentation?'*

I'm a bit of a rebel over visual aids. I will only use them, and recommend them to others, if I can control the technical environment and they are actively going to be helpful to the audience and myself.

Negotiation skills and tips

Regardless of whether you are buying or selling or seeking to develop some kind of collaborative joint venture you will, without doubt, find yourself in situations where you will need negotiation skills to succeed. Here are a few tips, traps and observations to bear in mind.

Who goes first?

This is one of those questions that always comes up, but unfortunately doesn't have an absolute definitive answer. The truth is your strategy might well vary according to the circumstances, how great your desire is to do a deal, and who you are negotiating with. Nevertheless let me express my opinion and a recommendation.

I used to recommend the standard approach of trying to get the other party to go first, in the hope that by seeing their cards, you could respond appropriately. Despite the logic of this, my experience indicates that this will rarely work to your advantage. In truth, I have personally had and witnessed much better results when going first. Let me explain why.

In real life, most negotiations always tend to revolve around the opening price or terms and generally end up reasonably close to them. The opening figure or terms generally seem to lay down a psychological marker and barrier around which the rest of the discussions take place. It is better for you to control and fix this.

Always try to negotiate

In my experience more things are negotiable than might at first sight seem obvious. My advice is always try to negotiate better terms or deals by being respectful and by asking questions.

In most situations, the worst-case scenario is that your attempt is turned down and you can revert to the original position.

Negotiation starts before the negotiating!

Most people think of negotiation as the haggling that goes on about the actual terms and financial arrangements of a particular transaction.

Remember, however, that before you get to the haggling stage it is most likely there would have been some ongoing discussions, meetings and information sharing. Always bear in mind that by asking the right questions at this early stage you may be able to gather valuable information which will be useful to you when it comes to the actual negotiation.

Do your homework

When it comes to negotiating, information is power. Find out as much as you can about alternatives, options, deals done with other parties, competitors, background circumstances and the people involved.

It is worth the effort and you never know what you might turn up that will be useful to you later on.

Be willing to walk away

Always decide in advance of any discussion or negotiation at what point you would cease to feel good and happy with the deal. If you can't do it within that range then you should not consider doing it at all.

Negotiate with questions

Instead of bluntly stating your position it can be much more effective to use questions, using the words 'if' and 'how'. For example:

■ *'How close are you able to get to X pounds?'*

■ *'If I were to agree to X, how flexible can you be with regard to Y?'*

Don't just negotiate in round figures!

It is very curious that the human mind seems to want to think and do business in round figures. If I open a negotiation at £1,000 and the counter offer is £800 there is a great psychological temptation to agree to meet in the middle and settle at £900.

What, however, is wrong with £949 or £873? Don't throw money away by thinking only in round figures.

Negotiation is not a contact sport

I have come across some people who can be extremely aggressive and confrontational in a negotiation and indeed enjoy the process because of the sense of power and control it gives them. Bear in mind that you may want to do business with that organisation or individual again and that, as in every other aspect of business life, word-of-mouth is hugely important.

What else other than money might be negotiable or traded?

When it comes to business deals, the focus, more often than not, is on money. Try asking, however, what other factors might become part of the negotiation. If you want to negotiate the price downwards you need to ask yourself: What else can I offer in return? You could ask:

- *'If I were to do such and such for you, would you help me with something else without any money changing hands?'*

- *'I'll tell you what, if I get it to you by tomorrow, would you be prepared to pay our initial asking price?'*

- *'If we were to promote your service to our customer base, how much of a discount would you offer us?'*

If I were in their shoes how would it feel?

By asking yourself this question you force your mind to respect the fact that the other person will want to feel good about the eventual deal. Your aim is not to get what you want at their expense, but to find a mutually beneficial solution that works for you both. So ask yourself these sorts of questions:

- How would I respond, if I were them?
- How important is this negotiation for them?
- What other possible options might they respond with?
- What are the benefits for them of my specific proposal?
- What is the deal that they will be hoping to do?
- What will make them feel good about the final outcome?
- What reasons might they have for turning me down?
- What questions might they want to ask me?

Time management skills and tips

So what has time management got to do with business development? It's simple. If you or your people are overstretched, stressed or spending time and resources doing the things that won't make a difference, then your business development results are likely to be adversely affected.

Here then are eight tips to keep in mind:

Control is everything

The key word is control. If you're not in control of your time, other people and circumstances are. Work, friends, families, colleagues, businesses, public bodies and technology all conspire to drain your time if you let them.

The key to gaining better control is planning. No, I am not talking about goal setting. Time planning is simply the process of actively thinking about what choices you are going to make about how you spend your time, in order to keep control and to accomplish whatever it is you want to do. There is one simple question you need to get used to asking: *'Who has or will have control over my time in this situation: is it me or someone else?'* If it is not you then you need to consider or plan how you can regain time.

Have you ever heard yourself using these expressions?

▨ *'Give me a call when you are ready.'*

▨ *'Let me know when you want to meet up.'*

▨ *'I don't mind whether you come to us, or if you like we'll travel to you.'*

▨ *'I'm clear all day, I can totally fit in with you.'*

Who do you think has control in these situations? Control is everything – planning is control.

Think outside of hour and half-hour blocks of time

Are you open minded and ready to consider something new? Read and think about this carefully until you fully understand it.

It is not so much a tip or a technique but something more powerful. It is to do with our personal relationship with time. It challenges the way we are unconsciously programmed to think about and use our time.

Let me explain by asking you a few questions:

▨ When you arrange business meetings, what times crop up in your diary more than others?

▨ When you set your alarm for the morning, what time do you set it for?

▨ When you make your evening social arrangements, what times do you typically allocate?

In the majority of cases, I bet the answers to these questions are at hourly or half-hourly units of time.

I have personally researched this and know for a fact that:

- 50 per cent of all time arrangements, plans and reminders are fixed on the hour;

- 40 per cent of all time arrangements, plans and reminders are fixed on the half hours;

- 10 per cent of all time arrangements, plans and reminders are fixed at other times and most of them are at the quarter-hour slots.

What this means in practice is that 90 per cent of people fix their business, professional, social and personal arrangements on the hour or on half-hour time blocks.

If people think and operate in this way, then we limit ourselves in terms of arranging and planning to the number of hour and half-hour units there are in the day or particular section of the day we are dealing with.

By doing this we literally write off huge chunks of time. Stop just thinking in these blocks of time and you will gain a massive amount of additional options and time.

Spend your business development time where it will have most impact – understand the 80/20 rule!

Let's face it, there will be elements of what you do that will produce fewer results than others. Doesn't it make sense therefore to spend your time on the components that will give you the best outcome?

There is a principle that states that 80 per cent of the effects or results come from just 20 per cent of the causes or input. For those of you who haven't come across this pearl of wisdom before, this is known as the Pareto Principle, named after an Italian economist who noted that 80 per cent of all property in Italy was owned by just 20 per cent of the population.

Look at the following examples to see where it applies in life generally:

- Have you ever noticed, if you're in business development, how 20 per cent of your efforts give you 80 per cent of your sales and revenue?

- In your social and personal life, isn't 80 per cent of your time spent with just 20 per cent of the people you know?

- Have you found out yet that 20 per cent of your family and friends give you 80 per cent of your headaches and problems?

By the way don't get too hung up on the precise statistics here. I may well be out by a few percentage points here and there with some of these examples, but the principle is absolutely valid.

Actively identify which of your daily business development activities give you the best results or outcomes and then spend more of your time doing those.

Master your habits ... master your time!

I have often observed people as they start their working day. Many are the victim of habits. What do they do?

■ Many have a coffee and read the paper for 10 minutes. If you do this ... why? Is it to ease you into the day? Is it because this is a priority activity that has to be done then? Is this a good or a bad habit? I am not saying you should or you shouldn't, but if you just do it because you always have ... then examine whether this behaviour is a positive use of that early and fresh moment of the day.

■ Many go through their post and e-mails. Why? Does this have to be done at that moment? What would happen if you did it later?

Regularly question why you do, what you do, when you do it.

Have a time planning system

I know people who live and manage their personal and business lives by accident rather than intent. Everything is urgent, mistakes are regularly made, some things are forgotten and many things are often left to the last minute and then done badly. Not a great state if you want to get great business development results.

I know some people hate detailed planning, but though the sophistication of the process is up to you, one thing is certain: any planning system is better than none. If you don't plan at all you won't have control over your life.

Let me give you my personal, simple, guiding principle to any planning methods. I call it the www question system approach to planning. It couldn't be simpler. Stick to it and you won't go far wrong. Each 'w' stands for an important question:

■ W = **What** do you 'have to' and 'want to' get done?

■ W = **When** will you do it?

■ W = **Where** will you write this information down so that it is easily visible and accessible to remind you?

The rest is detail!

Master your priorities

In order to plan your time and business development projects to get the maximum control, you need to make choices constantly about what to do first, next and where to spend your time to best effect.

With these thoughts in mind let me give you the absolute golden rule of prioritising: **do the most important thing first.**

Before you begin your day, consciously ask yourself the general question: what is the most important thing to do first? Once you have an answer then that is what you should do. Once that is done, you move on to the next most important task and so on. That way, when the day is done, if you have not completed everything, you have at least spent the bulk of your time on those things of most value.

So how do you decide what is the most important? Many time management 'gurus' have written about this question and offered some fixed and definitive answers. I don't like or believe that one answer works for everyone and in every situation, so here is a list of questions and criteria to help you decide on how to choose which is the most important, bearing in mind that there isn't a right or wrong choice. Ask yourself:

■ Which is the most unpleasant or toughest task so that I can get that out of the way first?

■ Which is the easiest and quickest?

■ Which can I do best to put myself in the most confident and positive state of mind to tackle the other things?

■ Which will make the biggest and most profound effect on my ultimate objective?

■ Which activity brings me closest to the money?

■ Which is the most urgent?

■ Which just 'feels' like the one to start with?

■ Which issue on the list is giving me the most anxiety or stress when I think about it?

■ Which of these, if it had to, could wait until tomorrow?

■ What choice might have an effect on other people?

■ What is most fun ... the thing that you have most been looking forward to doing?

■ Which of the tasks has the most pressing deadline?

■ What state of mind, mood or health do I need to be in to get certain things done?

■ What actual time makes the most sense to do specific things?

■ If something unexpected were to crop up ... which one couldn't wait?

■ Will it make a difference to the outcome and result when I do the task?

Focus your mind on each task and ask: What would the consequence be of not doing that particular thing today?

Master your e-mail

Many people quite reasonably complain about e-mail and information overload, but do absolutely nothing to limit the amount of time they waste handling the never-ending torrent of e-mails, 75 per cent of which are unwanted promotional junk. I have encountered many folk who have simply given up and accepted 'e-mail time loss' as a necessary evil of society. The good news is you don't have to.

You can't make the problem go away completely, but you can and should adopt a number of simple, damage-limitation strategies to minimise the effect. What you need to do is to ask: **What are the things relating to e-mail overload that I can control?** The answer is that there are several areas of activity that are partially within your personal sphere of influence:

■ Control how often and when you check your e-mails. You don't have to check every few minutes. Have a set time for this once or twice a day.

■ Control who is sending you e-mails. Get off unwanted lists.

■ Control when you send an e-mail. You don't have to respond immediately.

■ Control how you write the e-mail to minimise problems for the recipient. Often this will be reciprocated. If you write long chatty e-mails you are likely to get them back.

■ Control the IT tools you use to manage the process better. Make use of any tools you have on your computer for managing e-mails.

Master your meetings

If you want to find a way of wasting valuable business development time, have a meeting to discuss business development!

Have you ever been to a meeting, particularly an internal company one, where you left feeling uplifted and excited, like you had really achieved something useful and that this was a great use of your time? I have, but not often! I struggle to think of more than a few which have been necessary and totally constructive. There seems to be a culture in many organisations of simply holding meetings as a substitute for actually getting on with the job.

It never ceases to amaze me, how much time is squandered in meetings.

> I once attended a formal gathering of a major legal practice which had 20 partners present, all of whom charged about £250 per hour. The only issue to discuss was what percentage shade of grey their new brochure front cover should be printed in. This discussion went on for three hours. If you do a bit of basic number crunching, this vital meeting and decision cost them 60 hours of time and at their charging rate amounted to £15,000. Time and money well spent, don't you think?

It is astonishing and ironic that one of the things that business development people spend so much of their work time on is regarded, by them, as one of the biggest time traps of all.

Here are just a few of the comments I have heard when I have asked people about meetings in their organisation:

■ *'Given e-mail and other modern ways of communicating with each other, it is incredibly outdated to think that every time we need to speak to each other we have to have a meeting.'*

■ *'We have weekly business development meetings. Every time we virtually discuss the same things. We talk a lot and no one ever does anything.'*

■ *'On the whole I think business development meetings here are a waste of time. The only good thing about them is that I can stock up on sandwiches, fruit and chocolate biscuits.'*

Of course, the reality is that some meetings are productive and are absolutely justified. What is it then that differentiates the worthwhile from the time-wasting meetings? Here are a few tips on how to master your time when it comes to meetings.

TIPS ON MASTERING YOUR TIME SPENT IN MEETINGS

- Have very specific objectives.
- Cancel the meeting if key people are not there.
- Have as few people involved as possible.
- Have an agenda – a planned list of things to discuss.
- Have fixed start and end times.
- Don't arrange a meeting unless one is absolutely necessary.
- Don't travel to a meeting unless it is essential.
- Don't serve refreshments unless hospitality is a key part of the meeting.

'Meetings are indispensable when you don't want to do anything.'

John Kenneth Galbraith

9

Pulling it all together – making it happen

Let me ask you a ridiculous question that seemingly has nothing to do with business development. **There are three birds sitting on a fence. Two of them decide to fly away. How many are left?** The answer is three. Deciding to fly away is not the same as actually doing it.

Do you know the biggest single reason that business development efforts fail? The answer is simple: the inability to action the great ideas people have had.

Here are a few common scenarios that I have encountered on numerous occasions:

- organisations that hold monthly business development meetings, which sound the same every month but with very little action taking place between them;
- business people going on expensive business development courses or reading books like this one and getting all fired up, but then carrying on as before;
- getting business development and marketing gurus in to write 'the plan' and then having talked about it, leave it sitting on a shelf gathering dust.

Do any of these scenarios sound familiar in your organisation? Does your business suffer from 'activity inertia'?

With all this in mind then, here are a number of vital tips, some extreme pragmatism and commonsense advice to help you pull your business development ideas together. Some of them are the exact opposite of what you will find elsewhere, so read with care and an open mind.

Beware of planning madness

Planning is hugely important. You must plan *but* if you actually want to get anything vaguely constructive done, you must observe these rules when it comes to planning.

Keep the plan simple and short

I have already mentioned the need to avoid the over-complicated plan that sounds and looks great but that nobody can understand. Don't judge a plan by how thick it looks or how many pages it has. A 400-page document is almost certainly less effective than a 10-page summary, which sets out precisely what should be done, how, by whom, at what cost and with sensible and realistic targets.

Don't build your actions around planning meetings

Here is a hard and sad fact of corporate business life. The more planning meetings you have to have and the more people you involve in the process, the less you will get done. It is not smart to call a meeting to decide to do something that is obvious.

For example, I worked with an organisation which was losing large sums of money each month. I showed it why and it totally agreed and accepted the cause of the problem. The organisation, however, could not fix it straight away because its next scheduled business development planning meeting was not for another two months ... Sigh.

Know what to do first

One of the main causes of 'activity inertia' is businesses simply not knowing what to do first. If you have already read the rest of this book then this should not be a major problem for you. Your focus should be on 'Priority 1' ... converting your enquiries to profitable business. You should limit your investment of time and money on other activities until you have truly mastered this issue and plugged any leaks in your 'enquiries bucket'. (See Chapter 5.)

Create some 'have to' targets

Let me explain what I mean. Think of a time when you have been under pressure to get something done or achieve a particular outcome. Maybe you're going on holiday and you have to get something out of the way before you leave, or you have to get fit enough to participate in a particular event. Is it not the case that in most of those situations, when you were up against a compelling 'have to', you either met your deadline and targets and achieved your outcome or, if not, you got pretty close to it? Don't ask me how or why. We all seem to have some sort of built-in mechanism that enables us to stretch much further and achieve more, once we 'HAVE TO'!

The problem with many businesses with great ideas and business development ambitions is that there are often no fixed 'have to' targets. They simply set off with good intentions hoping for the best.

Well, I am going to give you some achievable 'have to' targets right now, which you can aim for and build your strategy and action around. They relate specifically to the business development priorities that have been a major theme throughout this book. So your 'have to' target over the next 12 months is:

- to increase the conversion rates of your leads and enquiries into business by 10 per cent;
- to increase the volume of business you get from existing customers and clients by 10 per cent. *This can either come from direct repeat or additional purchases from them, or from recommendations and introductions to others who buy ... or better still both;*
- to increase the number of new leads and enquiries coming in from external activities by 10 per cent.

I would also suggest you explore how you can increase your prices or fees in those areas that are possible by 10 per cent.

Take each of these 'have to' targets in turn and do what is necessary to achieve them. In many cases you will do better and in others the activity and focus will get you pretty close. By the way, you will not just be 10 per cent better off. The total percentage compounded growth in your business will be much greater and the financial benefits will be huge!

Hit your targets by working backwards

With those businesses which do set financial targets and goals, I have often felt that they are not activity led. All too often the target in any given business development plan is random and aspirational, without any supporting mechanism for getting there. Sometimes the target seems so hugely disproportionate that psychologically it seems unachievable. This then triggers the 'activity inertia' mentioned earlier.

With this in mind let me suggest a very simple mechanism, which I have used successfully on behalf of others and indeed for myself in a variety of ventures. It is the process of deciding on your goal and then working backwards, breaking it down into smaller targets that seem much more realistic.

> For example, suppose you operate a business that charges people a £30 per month subscription scheme for some service or product. Your goal is to generate an additional £100,000 per year.
>
> Getting to £100,000 may seem huge and almost impossible, but by breaking it down and working backwards, it looks like this.
>
> Ask yourself: 'How many new subscribers do I need to generate that £100,000?' Well, if a subscriber is paying £30 per month, then each subscriber contributes £360 worth of income. Thus to hit your £100,000 target, you need another 278 subscribers. Divide that by 52 to show how many you need to win on average each week and the answer is just over five.
>
> Your challenge and target then becomes, not 'How do I produce £100,000 of additional revenue?' but 'What do I have to do to simply get an extra five subscribers per week?'.

Simply by using the business development priorities concept in the right order that five becomes very achievable. Indeed, you may be able to get what you need just by relying on Priority 1 and converting more enquiries into business.

Provide strong leadership and involve others

Making the decisions is important but your team needs to see strong leadership, activity, commitment and enthusiasm from the very top of your operation for any business development efforts. Team members need to see that you are practising what you preach and that you are giving them the tools to achieve their targets, which might involve personal skills training.

Stop putting things off

There always seems to be a good reason why, *'Now is not a good time to take action.'* Here are a few of the ones I have heard:

- We've got quality consultants in.
- We are reviewing our computer systems.

- We are thinking about moving offices.
- We are recruiting some new people.
- We are having air conditioning installed.
- It's coming up to Christmas.
- The summer is a bad time to do things.
- It's hard to motivate people in the cold, dark, winter months.
- We are having a new accounts system installed.

There may well be some valid logic behind all of these. However, in my experience, if you wait for the perfect time, you may wait for ever and do nothing.

'You may never know what results come of your action, but if you do nothing there will be no result.'

Mahatma Gandhi

Conclusion

As you come to the end of *The Financial Times Guide to Business Development,* I hope you have had several of those 'that's it' moments, when something has just clicked in your mind and you realise what you have been missing and what you should do now. I also hope that as you have read through the ideas, tips and techniques you have smiled once in a while.

At its simplest, business development success is all about:

- getting the simple and basic things in place to begin with;
- constantly keeping them under observation;
- asking the right business questions;
- getting your business development priorities right;
- focusing on personal performance business development skills;
- having the determination, wisdom and stamina to take sustained action.

If you do all these things, then you are well on the way to business development success.

Finally, remember two things:
1 Every single thing a business does has a potential impact on business development.
2 It's the customers and clients who pay the bills!

'Every morning in Africa a gazelle awakens knowing it must today run faster than the fastest lion or it will be eaten. Every morning a lion awakens knowing it must outrun the slowest gazelle or it will starve. It matters not whether you are a gazelle or a lion, when the sun rises you had better be running.'

African proverb

Index